Ain't this Romantic!?!

Ain't this Romantic!?!

by Kent Hanawalt

With bonus section of cowboy stories
contributed by
Kenny Doig

This is a non-fiction work. All the names and places are real, and the events are laid out exactly as I remember them.

Printed in the USA by
CreateSpace.com

Version 1.2 - February 2012

Kent Hanawalt
McLeod, Montana
westboulderpublishing@gmail.com

Dedicated to my wife Kathi
and my mother Imogene

without whose support, encouragement,
and downright prodding
this book would never have been printed.

Introduction

"Ain't this romantic?" hollered Steve from his position on the opposite flank of the handful of cattle we were struggling to push into the biting wind.

"The best part is that there are no mosquitoes," I replied, pulling my neck-scarf up to cover my numbing cheeks.

Steve Gordon and I were gathering a small group of two-year-old heifers with new calves which had been caught in an open field by a late winter storm. The heifers were new to this business of motherhood and alternately ran away from the group in a tizzy, then returned bawling for their new babies. The calves couldn't decide whether to follow the group, their mothers, the horses, or to just lay down where they were and hide.

Our objective was to push the group into the shelter of the brush along lower Richardson Creek, but our erratic progress was further hampered by a north wind which was blowing snow into our faces at a temperature of 5° below zero.

The life of a cowboy has long been envisioned as romantic. Popular movies of the late 1980s, such as "Urban

Cowboy" and "Lonesome Dove", sparked a resurgence of interest in the cowboy way of life, and commercial "trail drives" became popular recreational events. Steve and I are "real" cowboys, making our living day in and day out from the cattle for which we are responsible. We both understand that modern ranch life has become largely mechanized, and that a cowboy now spends more time jockeying equipment than riding horses.

But for each of us, horses continue to be vital to our lifestyle and self-image. We know both the joys and sorrows of the ranching business, and our love is unshaken. We tolerate the months of routine and boring chores, and live for the moments of drama and excitement.

In these pages I share some of the events that have made cowboy life worthwhile for me. I hope you enjoy reading them as much as I have enjoyed living them.

Ain't this Romantic!?!

Rolling Ropers

There were three of us riding in the front of the pickup this beautiful spring day on the east slope of the Bear Paw Mountains of Montana. It was calving time on the Mitchell Ranch and we had just finished feeding the cow/calf pairs. Doug, Mark, and I were headed back toward the buildings for dinner when someone noticed a cow in need of attention.

The cow had not "cleaned" after calving - the placenta had not been expelled. This is not an uncommon occurrence, but it must be treated. A cow left alone will likely develop a uterine infection that can leave her very ill, and probably barren. Treatment involves donning a long veterinary obstetrical glove to clean out the putrid material, and insert antibiotic boluses.

We were in a big bunch of cows, a couple of miles from the barn. Doug, the boss, considered the time it would take to drive home, catch and saddle horses, ride back out and find the cow, then take her back to the barn - versus roping her here and now.

We checked out the pickup for the necessary supplies: behind the seat were lariats; under the seat was a box of gloves; in the jockey box was a jar of antibiotic boluses. We had all the equipment, and the cow was in sight.

The decision was made. I raised questioning eyebrows at my brother Mark as each of us took a rope and climbed into the back. Doug put the rig in gear, and off we went after the cow.

A good rope horse will put you right up on a critter, and follow at an appropriate distance. He can keep the roper within range wherever the cow chooses to go. A pickup has enough speed, but nowhere near the agility of an animal. And pickups don't maneuver well the various obstructions indigenous to prairie pastures.

Another advantage of a horse is in the stability of the rider. Sitting astraddle the horse and having two stirrups for balance is considerably less precarious than standing in the bed of a moving pickup.

But Doug pulled in beside the cow as Mark and I swung our loops. When she saw us coming, the old girl sensed danger and headed off at a high lope. As the pickup closed the gap, we each took a swing and a miss, and watched as the cow ducked off to the left. There was just enough time for us to brace as Doug swung around for another pass at our quarry.

The cow was on to our game now, and the next time around she was quicker on the dodge. We weren't as close to the cow as we'd have been ahorseback, and we were off at a bad angle. Both our loops came up empty again.

We were coming up behind the cow for the third time and gaining, when Mark hollered and Doug hit the brakes. We were thrown against the cab as the pickup slid to a stop just short of an irrigation ditch.

It took awhile to find a crossing suitable for a pickup, and get over to where the cow was now standing - time enough for her catch her breath for the next heat of the race.

We made several more runs with much the same results. As soon as we were close enough for a throw, the rig would have to swerve around a rock or a bush, or the cow would duck off to the side and lose us. Mark and I in the back were fighting to stay aboard our wildly gyrating "steed".

Finally Mark connected with a loop. Then we were faced with another problem - there was no saddle horn on which to dally.

Roping technique has two basic divisions - "dally" roping, or "hard and fast". Rodeo calf ropers tie hard and fast: the end of the rope is knotted to the horn. Team ropers in a rodeo use the dally method - once the loop is in place on an animal, the cowboy jerks up the slack and takes a turn around the horn to hold it.

In some parts of the country, all roping is done hard and fast. "If I catch it, I keep it" is the rallying cry of the proponents of that method. This allows the rider to leave his horse and go down the rope to the calf.

The prairie ropers of Montana mostly use the dally style of roping. The word "dally" comes from the Spanish "dar le vuelta", meaning "give the turn". The originators of the dally technique were the old Spanish Vaqueros. Their rawhide lariats were not strong enough to take the jerk of a heavy animal, so they had to "play" the rope, much like a fisherman landing a big catch. Vaqueros used long ropes, and played the slack around the broad wooden horns of their Spanish style saddles.

With no saddle horn on which to "give a turn", we scrambled to get the end of the rope secured to something solid before it pulled through our hands. Finding the spare tire rack in the pickup box, we quickly threaded the rope through and made a knot.

When the lariat was tied off, we hollered for Doug to stop. After bringing the pickup to a halt, Doug opened his door to step out. But he quickly changed directions as he saw the trajectory of the angry cow! Doug was on his way out the off-side door when the cow hit. Her weight folded the open driver's door forward into the front fender, nearly tearing it off its hinges.

Doug kept glancing back at the deformed cab as we worked at catching the cow's hind legs. But we were again faced with the disadvantage of being without a horse. In order to "heel" a critter it is necessary for the legs to be moving. A horse can pull

3

an animal in a circle while the heeler lays the trap-loop to pick up the hind legs.

The cow was hot, tired, and angry. She was secured to the pickup with thirty feet of nylon lariat. Whenever one of us would come near her with a second rope, the cow would charge.

Finally, Mark went out as a decoy while I maneuvered into position behind the cow. When the mad mamma charged Mark, I was able to flip a loop into position to catch her hind legs.

With a critter squirming on one end, the heel rope must be kept tight. If the loop is allowed to loosen, the animal will kick free. From a saddle, a man can take a turn around his rubber covered horn and let the horse's weight do all the work. From the ground, holding onto a rope affixed to the back end of an angry 1200 pound cow is quite a struggle.

The process of catching that cow had burned a lot of time and energy. We had chased her over hill and dale before the final hand-to-hand combat. By the time we had the cow immobilized, the offending afterbirth had dropped free. We had only to insert the antibiotic boluses to complete the task that we had begun a half hour earlier.

It took some prying to get the mangled door shut. Doug was quiet as we drove home for dinner, and we were respectfully sober. As long as that pickup was on the ranch it would be a constant reminder of the foolishness of trying to save time by using a pickup to do the job of a horse.

H-Heifers

My brother, Mark, and I had both been raised among our grandfather's livestock. We each loved horses, and had found our way to real horse country in the Bear Paw Mountains of North Central Montana where we were eager to become accepted.

Mitchell Ranch had been Mark's first experience. He had hired on for calving, and took to the lifestyle instantly. Spring had sprung and the grass was starting to come when I joined him there at the tail end of the calving season.

Working together was a first for the two of us, and we were enjoying it. That was quite a change from our growing up years when we were constantly at each others' throats. I'd always considered my little brother to be a pretty rotten kid as we were growing up, and I was surprised at how well he'd turned out.

One day we went off in a pickup to feed the bunch that Mark called the "auterial heifers".

Heifers is the term for young female cattle - usually aging through three years old, when they are finally considered to be "cows". Most breeds of cattle achieve maturity at about four years of age. Heifers are generally bred as yearlings to bear their first calves when they are two years old - two years before they have grown to their full size.

This class of cattle has different requirements than the rest of the cow herd and is thus usually managed separately. The smaller body size of the heifers results in a much higher incidence of difficulty giving birth. They need more and better feed since their bodies are still growing at the same time they are providing milk for their new calves. And the older cows often push the younger ones away from feed.

I had majored in animal science in college, and I'd been working full time on Montana ranches for a couple of years, and I'd never heard the term "auterial" before. I asked Mark about it. He'd heard Lawrence Mitchell use the words, he explained, and had followed suit without questioning.

"That must mean they haven't had a calf before," Mark guessed.

I wasn't satisfied with that definition, but I didn't have a dictionary to check it out. I mulled the word over in the back of my mind and waited for the chance to follow up on its meaning. It was a few days later when I had the opportunity to question Lawrence directly.

A puzzled look came over his face when I asked Lawrence the meaning of the word "auterial". He thought for a few moments as he tried to make a connection in his own mind.

His brow furrowed as he tried to figure out what I was talking about. Finally he replied in his typical stuttering fashion: "Ah… you mean, ah… ah two-year-ol' heifer?"

Blizzard!

April 15, 1973 began as a beautiful spring day in the Bears Paw Mountains. The sun was spending more time in Montana now, after wintering somewhere farther south. The color of the prairie was rapidly changing from the bleached brown of last year's grass as the new shoots of green pushed through and took over.

I'm not much of a tractor man, but I had agreed to plow a small field not too far from where my growing family was camped. I usually get quickly bored with the driving around and around in circles that makes farming, but the view today kept my mind occupied.

Overhead was a clear blue sky. Underneath lay fresh-turned earth. Behind me were the crisp, clean mountains. Ahead of me, across the prairie and on the other side of the Fort Belknap Reservation, was the outline of the Little Rockies.

At noon my ears were relieved as I shut down the noisy diesel contraption and walked the half mile home for dinner. Fresh antelope steaks were cooking on the wood stove in the abandoned bunkhouse that we had reclaimed from the mice. I sat down at the table and pulled Amy, my year-old daughter, up onto my lap. My wife Barbara put some dishwater on the stove to heat.

The big south-facing windows of the bunkhouse let in a lot of light. This was an important feature of the building as there was no electricity. The main house had been sold and moved off the foundation several years before; the power poles had been used to build a shed. We did have "running" water of a sorts - it was running <u>by</u> in a little stream.

7

As the noon hour passed, clouds gathered between us and the sun. The light coming through the windows became less and less. By the time I was ready to go back to the farming, the wind had turned cold, and snow was coming out of those clouds! I never did like to drive tractor, and this weather was all the excuse I needed to quit for the day.

The wind and snow escalated all afternoon as I scurried around to find a few more fence posts to saw for the fire. By morning there were 3-foot drifts and visibility of about 20 feet.

For three days we sat by the fire and watched the storm rage. We'd have liked to get up to the ranch headquarters to take a shower and wash clothes, but it would be foolhardy to set out in this weather. Evenings were mighty short and the nights long without electricity to augment the meager light coming in the windows.

On the morning of the fourth day the wind began to lose its fury. The snow eased up and visibility improved. By noon the sun was again shining over the prairie. We were still thinking how nice a hot shower would feel, but our two-wheel-drive pickup would never make it through the drifts that had piled up downwind of every rock, bush, and tree.

Suddenly I heard the roar of exhaust as a pickup clawed its way into the yard, chains on all four wheels. "Grab your coat and your overboots", said the driver, "We've got a hell of a mess at the home place."

As we headed back toward the headquarters I looked all around at the landscape. Drifts were everywhere, the coulees full of snow. The ridges had blown almost clear, leaving patches of frosted grass. Cows and calves stood in bunches here and there, all of them bawling. A tractor was plowing over, under, around, and through the drifts to break trail for the pickup following in its tracks with a load of hay.

We picked our way where the snow seemed the most shallow, gunning through the spots where it had piled up deeper, and found our way to a haystack. Surveying the stack we found the easiest access and used our scoop-shovels to clear a path in.

Leaving the stack with a load of hay, we were soon met by a noisy crowd of hungry cows. In the storm, the cattle had drifted with the wind into the fence corners. They had been standing with empty bellies for three days, humped up and shivering with the cold. Now the cows were famished, and the hay disappeared as fast as we could haul it out to them.

The hair on a cow, even in the winter, is rather sparse. It could never be considered "fur" as on a bear. In cold weather, cattle depend on the heat generated by the digestion of the roughage in their diet.

A good ranch practice is to lay in a supply of straw for the winter. During arctic weather, a cow will consume twice the feed that she needs in nice weather. Straw does not have much food value, and is therefore relatively cheap. But the inefficiency of digestion is an excellent heat source, and the leftovers make a wonderful bedding to insulate the animals from the frozen earth.

But the winter was past, and most of the year's feed had been fed. The stacks of hay were dwindling.

We put off a couple of loads of hay before we saddled our horses. Cows were stranded here and there by the deep snow. We broke trail in to each little bunch and then pushed the cows over to where hay was spread. By dark we finally had all the cattle gathered to the feed-grounds. I took a pickup and followed our tracks back home. After supper and a sponge bath, I fell into bed exhausted.

The next day dawned clear and bright. The spring sun was much higher in the sky than it had been during the winter, and it glared off the new snow. Feeding the cows was much easier now

9

that we had trails opened up, and it only took us until noon. After dinner we were a horseback again.

As we fed we had noticed lots of hungry calves, and an equal number of cows with tight udders. Many of the pairs had been separated in the storm and the calves had not sucked in days. Cows identify their calves by smell. A number of the cows had either forgotten their calves, or the distinctive odor of their offspring had been overpowered by other smells in the crush of bodies during the storm. Anxious mamas and babies were bawling in every direction.

There was no way to know which one of the 1200 cows was the mother to any particular starving calf. Four of us rode until we found a bawling calf, gaunt and hungry. Then one of us would rope him and tie him down in the pickup driven by Grandma Rose while the others looked through the herd for swollen udders. Spotting a cow who hadn't been sucked, a pair of us would swing in behind and rope her down. Using rope braided from bale twine, we hobbled her hind legs together, and pushed the motherless calf up to suck.

Most of these newly-orphaned calves were a little head-shy. They had been kicked off before when they had tried to steal a meal from other cows. After a few tentative motions, however, the calves quickly went to work on the udder of the immobilized cow. In the meantime, someone would have found another calf who needed a mother, and the process was repeated.

At suppertime I again longed for a nice hot shower. But this would not be a possibility for awhile - the power lines in to the ranch had been blown down in the storm. In fact, supper would be a problem for those at the ranch headquarters. While my family had the dubious luxury of a wood stove, two of the three kitchens at the home place sported modern electric ranges!

Automatic forced air heating systems had likewise replaced the less efficient but simpler modes of heating in the newer homes. Our wood stove required a fair amount of labor to saw and split the fuel, but it continued to serve us well when others around us were trying to heat their homes and cook their meals with a fireplace. When I returned home I informed my wife of the good fortune of our independence from electricity.

On the third day after the storm, Doug's father, Lawrence, left us to battle the drifts and feed the cows without him. He took some warm clothes, a scoop-shovel, and his checkbook, and headed up the road toward town. It took three hours of plowing through the small drifts and shoveling through the large ones to make the five miles to the wide spot in the road called Cleveland. But the snowplows from Chinook hadn't yet reached there. After a little gossip and couple of drinks at the Cleveland Bar, Lawrence headed back to the ranch.

Again the next day Lawrence tried the county road. He arrived home after dark with a heavy load on his pickup. In the box was a tractor-mount snowblower. Trailing from the hitch was PTO-driven generator.

Before retiring for the night, the men attached a tractor to the generator and connected the output to the electric panel of Lawrence's house. For the first time in a week they had electricity to run the lights, the furnaces, and the pumps!

The next morning the generator was moved to the panel of Doug's house. During her eight hour shift of electrical service, Doug's wife, Joanne, washed the past week's accumulation of laundry, and cooked us a fine dinner. Mid-afternoon the generator went back to Lawrence. At bedtime the generator moved again. The night shift went to the two big freezers up in the shop.

And so the power was parceled at the ranch for two more weeks while utility crews worked long hours replacing miles of downed poles.

Meanwhile we continued to find calves that had been weaned in the storm. Each of the three milk cows was given four calves. Twenty-five more calves were fed with bottles. A five-gallon butterchurn was used twice a day to mix up milk replacer for the orphan calves.

The milk cows were fun to watch. After several days of being forced to let the strange calves suck, the cows claimed all four of the calves assigned to each of them. The cow would call her brood and smell each one before going out from the barn to graze. The experts say a cow can't count, but these old girls always knew when one of their four was missing.

Pleasant weather returned quickly and began to turn the snow into mud. But the snow wasn't gone soon enough to prevent a new problem: sun-burned udders.

We tried to keep the cows in areas where the snow was tramped down, but they liked to range off in search of the tender new shoots of grass. The bright spring sun reflecting off the snow caused the bags of lighter colored cows to become cracked and tender. Now we were roping cows for the purpose of greasing their teats.

And then we ran low on hay. The extra feed required by the late storm had emptied the stackyards of bales. One morning I was given a pitchfork.

I had seen some structures from afar which I had taken to be straw-roofed sheds. The sides were made of slab-wood, and a black thatch was visible on top. When we got closer I discovered that there were no open sides. These were old stacks of loose hay surrounded by slab-wood panels.

Pulling open the panels we found tightly compacted mounds covered with a musty, weathered scab. Under this crust we found beautiful green hay! These stacks had been there when the Mitchells bought the ranch seven years before. They had shrunk to half their original height, but six inches down the hay was just as clean and nutritious as the day is was stacked ten years before.

We continued to feed loose hay every morning until we had the last stack cleaned up. Our afternoon work included the job of roping cows to cut off the rope hobbles that were no longer necessary.

By the middle of May even the deepest drifts were gone. The moisture was quickly absorbed into the earth, to come back up in the form of grass. The country was green and lush, the air balmy. It was hard to believe how fierce the weather had been just a month before!

Choking!

I had driven up to the ranch headquarters that morning, where I saddled my horse for the day's work. At noon I was closer to home than to headquarters so I just rode in and tied up for dinner with my small family. My wife met me at the door.

"Thank God you're here! Amy is choking!"

My first-born daughter was just over a year old and of course stuffed into her mouth whatever her little fingers could grasp.

"She was playing with a penny and now she is choking on it!

I rushed in to assess the situation. Indeed the toddler was in distress – something was lodged in her throat.

My horse was tied nearby, and the pickup was 3 miles away. Red was half Quarter Horse and half Arabian. He was good and hard, and up for whatever mission. We galloped all the way to the ranch.

Holding the reins and barging through the door, I hollered to my brother that Amy was choking. I left the horse in his care, jumped in the pickup, and raced back down the trail from whence I had just come. It was smoother to be on this "road" ahorseback, and nearly as fast, but we would need the speed of a motorized vehicle when we finally reached the highway.

My wife was frantic with fear when I at last returned with the pickup. Amy was still in distress, gagging repeatedly on the coin lodged in her throat. We bounced along toward town as fast as the road conditions would allow, finally hitting the pavement when we reached the "town" of Cleveland – which entailed a two-room school and a post office.

Now on the oil road I could finally stomp on the throttle, hitting the top speed for this 1953 Chevy pickup – a mere 65 MPH.

Amy continued to gag as we raced up the road toward the town of Chinook. There was a doctor there, and I had located his office the previous winter when I had jabbed a stick into my thigh in a horse-wreck.

We were halfway to town when Amy – exhausted by more than an hour of pain and wretching, finally fell asleep on her mother's shoulder. Soon after she fell asleep, Amy swallowed, and the gagging was suddenly relieved. It seemed that as soon as she relaxed the penny was able to pass on down her throat.

The emergency was over by the time we reached town. We had the doctor examine her, and confirmed by x-ray that the coin had passed into her stomach. He assured us that it would most likely pass through into her diaper in just a few days.

It was in my Emergency Medical Technician advanced airway training years later that I learned in detail the anatomy of what we commonly refer to as the "throat". Within the neck are two tubes: along the front of the neck is the trachea – through which we breathe; and immediately behind it is the esophagus – through which we swallow.

In retrospect, I can see clearly that the penny was lodged in the esophagus, causing the "gagging" reflex. It was indeed uncomfortable, and would prevent food from passing through, but it was not an emergency. Air was still flowing freely through the trachea. But hindsight does you no good when you are faced with an emergency a long way from help.

Bear Paw Branding

With calving finished and the farming all done, the next major task was branding the calves. We had cut out the pairs from the calving fields into 3 bunches of 400 cows each. Branding those cattle was spread over three days - one day for each bunch.

We began the day by setting up a circle of portable corral panels in the corner of the field where the day's gather was pastured, leaving a large opening along one fence line. Rigs began to arrive from neighboring ranches at about 9:00, and we saddled up to gather the field.

When the pairs were all in the corral, a couple of ropes were hooked to the end of the corral, and horses helped drag the panels into a tighter circle, overlapping several lengths to make a 16 foot wide alley leading out of the corral. The cows were eager to escape, and a couple of guys afoot in the alley were able to let them past while turning the calves back into the corral. A couple of the better ropers were positioned at the exit to catch any calves that snuck past the men doing the sorting.

On one of these days I found myself in the middle of the alley, in precisely the right place to begin sorting out the cows.

The cows were eager to get out of the confines of the corral we had thrown up on the prairie. They had lost track of their calves in the shuffle and were determined to get back to the place they had last seen them. Ordinarily it would have been left to more experienced members of the crew to do the cutting, but I just happened to be in the wrong place at the wrong time.

I stepped back to let a stream of cows blow past me and out the opening in the circle of panels. When I saw a calf coming, I simply stepped forward and turned him back. A step backwards let more cows run out, and a step forward turned back more calves.

I had never considered myself a dancer, but that's what I was doing right there in front of God and all the neighbors – dancing with a bunch of cows.

The cows were flowing well, and was able to turn back every one of the calves. As the corral emptied, some of the men ahorseback worked the last of the cows toward the opening. The flow slowed, and finally stopped as the last cow ran down the make-shift sorting alley.

With the cows now on the outside and the calves on the inside, we pulled the corral into a smaller circle and set up the propane branding pot near the throat. While the irons began to heat, and the syringes were filled, the rest of us made our first trip to the ice chests. When the irons were deemed hot enough, the boss raised an arm and made a circling motion with his wrist, and the first three ropers went in.

These ropers rode into the bunch, standing a loop just ahead of a calf's hind legs. As the calf stepped forward, the roper pulled his slack, dallied to the saddle horn, and turned for the fire. Four teams of wrestlers were waiting. A team would step out and throw the calf on its side while the horse pulled past, drawing the calf into a good position near the fire.

When the wrestlers had the calf on the ground they pulled off the heel-rope and awaited the convergence of the rest of the ground crew. Castration of bull-calves, dehorning, vaccinations, and branding were accomplished. In an hour we were through the first 100 head, and the women showed up with dinner in the pickup.

I had been working with my brother Mark for the last couple of months, and we naturally paired off to wrestle. We had a good system and we were enjoying the work. Our strategy was to take opposite sides of the rope as a horse came between us. One of us would take the rope and the other the tail, pulling in opposite directions to throw the calf. When the calf reached the fire, one of us sat on the ground behind the calf holding tight to one hind leg and bracing a foot into the hock of lower leg, while the other of us kneeled with one knee on the calf's neck, pulling back on a front leg. It worked well for us and required a minimum of effort on our part. The country was pretty, the weather was nice, and there was an endless supply of beer.

Better than wrestling, however, was roping – and we looked for our opportunity to get in there ahorseback. All it took was short run where the wrestling was going a little faster than the roping and one of us would tighten our cinches and ride in to start heeling. Depending on how hot my roping was for the day, I could heel around 25 calves before I got tired enough to relinquish to another roper.

In the 70s most ranches were feeding small square bales and we loaded them all by hand. It took more labor to run a ranch in years past. Town jobs didn't have the same appeal that they seem to now, and the country had plenty of young men like Mark and I to do the wrestling. The girls from the neighboring ranches attended also, and the brandings were a social occasion as well as exchange of labor.

There were 4 of us working on the Mitchell ranch. A good branding crew required 3 roping, 8 wrestling, 2 vaccinating, 2 branding, 1 castrating, 1 dehorning, and a few for spares and consultations.

For 3 days in early June we had some 15 of the neighbors helping us brand, and it took another 10 days of branding on other ranches to repay the help. So for two weeks we were at a branding nearly every day.

When the brandings were finished it was time to move the cattle to summer range on the reservation – we had been ahorseback every day while we were calving in March and April, and here was another week spent exclusively atop our horses. It wouldn't be long until we turned out the horses and began the greasy, dusty, and boring job of riding the haying equipment. But for now we were cowboys, and we were enjoying every minute!

Stampede!

Ahead of us the bawling cattle moved eagerly eastward away from the shelter of their winter range on the east slopes of the Bears Paw Mountains. In the lead were the older cows who had made the trip many summers. We four riders enjoyed the sunshine on our backs and the new grass beneath the horses' feet as we kept the stragglers up with the bunch.

Snow still lay in the sheltered spots, the soggy remains of a late spring storm. After the biting cold of winter and the steady grind of calving, we felt the tension leave our bodies as our horses worked back and forth under the huge, blue Montana sky, pushing the cows onward across the prairie.

Although we'd been ahorseback all our lives, my brother Mark and I were enjoying the experience of trailing this herd of 400 pairs from the Mitchell Ranch in the Bear Paws to summer range on the Fort Belknap reservation. Lawrence Mitchell, who was approaching retirement age, was on the left flank of the herd. His adult son Doug was keeping the cattle shaped up on the right.

A jet passing high overhead was in sharp contrast to us on the ground. While he burned hundreds of gallons of fuel and covered thousands of miles, we burned only grass and hoped to cover but a few miles. Our concern was not speed, but rather to reach the Rattlesnake holding field with as little commotion as possible. Cows and calves will inevitably be separated in the confusion of a moving herd, and we had been as gentle as possible.

We moved along at such a steady pace that we reached the gate into the section pasture before we realized the morning was past. The cows headed for the creek for a drink, then turned back through the herd in search of their calves. The bawling quieted as the calves mothered up and eagerly began to suck.

After five hours in the saddle it felt good to swing down and head towards the pickup which had just arrived with our lunch. Doug and Lawrence dropped their reins and loosened cinches while Mark and I tied up to the pickup grill guard and reached for a cup of hot coffee. As the cows spread out to graze, we dug into the grub box and made short work of the lunch that Lawrence's wife Rose had brought. Then we dropped into the grass to give our stomachs a chance to settle.

The field in which we had stopped was called the Rattlesnake holding field by the Mitchells. It was one section in size - one mile square - 640 acres, and it was located within sight of the remains of the abandoned town of Rattlesnake.

In some parts of the world, 640 acres is a wealth of land. But not on the Montana plains. In this area it takes between 20 and 40 acres of grass to summer a cow. During the early part of this century thousands of families starved out of 320 acre prairie homesteads. The town of Rattlesnake had once been a center of commerce for the homesteaders of this area. But the hulls of the few remaining buildings were now the home of only the rattlesnakes themselves, and other assorted local wildlife.

This section field could support only about 40 pairs through a season; the 1200 that Mitchells owned would reduce the entire field to dust in just a few short weeks. Most of the cattle grazed on reservation allotments through the summer. This field was used mostly as a stopping place for the several groups of cattle that were trailed through to the reservation in June, and home again in the fall. We would pause here with three herds of around 400 pair before the month was ended.

After our "picnic" lunch, I dozed on the grass in the shade of the pickup. But when I heard Lawrence holler "Boots and

Saddles!" I jerked my head up in time to see a handful of calves emerge from the head of a coulee behind us. Mark's horse picked this precise time to kick a fly off his belly and hang a hind foot in his loose flank cinch. The horse reared back in surprise, breaking reins and cinch in one thrust, while spooking my horse which was tied beside him. Mark's saddle rolled under the horse's belly, adding fuel to the fire as both our mounts stampeded through the peaceful cattle. Doug and Lawrence ran to their horses to turn the bunch quitters, Doug never pausing to pull on his boots.

Mark and I were thankful to be in a field that was only a mile square as we ran over the hill after our horses, carrying the remains of our reins. We were panting and sweaty - as were the horses - when we finally got them cornered and caught. After repairing our gear, my brother and I turned our attention to the scattering cattle. A substantial number of calves had not yet found their mothers and were heading back to where they'd last sucked early that morning. Doug and Lawrence were out of sight, pursuing calves that had already headed back toward the ranch.

As we worked back and forth on tired horses, we were losing ground to the bawling animals. Finally, we let ourselves out the gate and raced up and down outside the fence, turning back the calves trying to crawl through and return to the only home they had ever known.

As the afternoon progressed, the cows gradually picked up their calves and bedded down, leaving just a few distressed mamas. It was then that Mark and I began to wonder what had happened to the rest of the crew. As the last calf in the field found a mother, we climbed off our weary mounts and discussed the situation.

The original plan had been to leave the horses in the Rattlesnake tonight and go on with the herd tomorrow. But now maybe they were waiting for us to ride back to the ranch. With no way to communicate with the rest of the crew we were at a loss as to what we should do - so we just waited.

The sun was low in the sky when Doug returned in the pickup with several calves hog-tied in the back. Their bawling attracted some anxious cows, and it wasn't long before the calves were all paired up and sucking.

We threw our saddles into the pickup and turned the horses loose with a pile of oats in the grass. On the ride home with Doug we learned what had happened "in the mean time, back at the ranch".

Having no piggin' strings and but one lariat between them, Lawrence and a stocking-footed Doug had pursued the escaped calves back to the field where we'd gathered that morning. When Rose arrived with the pickup and Doug's boots, they'd quit their played-out horses and began roping calves out the back of the pickup.

When Doug swerved to miss a ditch, Lawrence had fallen out on his head and was knocked cold. While Mark and I were holding the calves on the prairie, Doug and Rose had been speeding the unconscious Lawrence up the canyon and through the mountains to the hospital, 55 long, rough miles away.

The next morning, Doug's wife filled in for Lawrence as we pushed the cows on the last leg of their journey to summer range. As we rode along, I vowed to be more careful where and how I tied my horse; Mark pulled the slack out of his flank cinch; while Doug made a mental note to keep his boots on. And back home, Lawrence adjusted the ice pack on his head and swore to *drive* the pickup next time they tried to use it instead of a horse.

Shooting Gallery

The Bear Paw Mountains are prime country for cows - and therefore, cowboys. It is a region of mostly open, grass-covered hills punctuated by rocky outcroppings and stands of pine. The meadows are fertile, water is abundant, and there is adequate cover for both cattle and wildlife.

Antelope frequent the flatter areas of the Bear Paws; both Whitetail and Mule Deer cling closer to the protection of mountain, tree, and bush. There is the occasional Black bear, and plenty of coyote. Sage Hens, Prairie Chickens, and Hungarian Partridge are everywhere, as well as Chinese Ringneck Pheasants.

Fall in the Bear Paws, like nearly every other region of Montana, brings out the hunters in droves. There is always plenty of game there for all comers, and most ranchers welcome hunters onto their land. The owners of the Mitchell Ranch, where I was employed, were no exception. They had already fielded numerous phone calls and were expecting a couple of dozen hunters to spread out over their thousands of acres on opening day.

Lawrence Mitchell and I had discussed the situation in advance, and worked out our own plan for opening day. Nearly all of the hunters out from town would be afoot. We expected that when the shooting started at dawn on opening morning there would be hundreds of deer looking for a place to hide.

Black butte stuck up just behind the ranch headquarters - a pile of volcanic rock fringed with a stand of pine. The slope of the butte was rather steep, and was comprised of dinner-plate sized slide-rock that was miserable to navigate. The pine grove on top gave a perfect hiding place for nimble-footed deer, offering a good view of the approach of any foe.

The deer would be out grazing the hayfields at first light, we reasoned, and would be startled at the sudden invasion of their domain by the sight and smell of enemies from every direction. Black Butte was the obvious place for a number of deer to escape, and if we were to arrive there under the cover of darkness, the other hunters would drive the deer right to us.

Last thing before supper on Saturday we used a pickup to run the horses in from pasture. Each of us picked his favored mount for the expedition and fed them grain while we turned the rest of the bunch back out to grass. Our plan for tomorrow was for both of us to be back at the horsebarn by coffee time with nice young bucks draped over our saddles.

On Sunday morning Lawrence and I each arose earlier than usual. When I had finished my breakfast I walked across the yard to join him and Rose for coffee. As we nursed our cups of fresh hot brew we saw the headlights of several pickups pulling into the yard and heard the sound of doors being slammed.

There was just a hint of light in the east as I walked with Lawrence to the horsebarn. We quickly haltered our horses and let them munch on another bait of oats as we threw on our saddles and drew up the cinches. It took a little rigging with bale twine to sling the thermos safely on a saddle, but we intended to enjoy our little morning excursion.

When we at last switched off the barn lights and headed out, we were surprised at how quickly the sky had brightened. The outline of Black Butte was already visible to the west.

It was only a mile or so from the buildings across the hayfields to the base of the butte, and it was a glorious fall morning. Looking around us as we rode, we could see spots of fluorescent orange in several directions.

Daylight comes quickly to the clear and open Big Sky of Montana - a little quicker than we expected. The pair of us were not yet to the base of the Butte when shooting erupted to the north of us.

As we searched the terrain in the direction of the first shots we heard more rifle fire to the south. Soon we spotted a bunch of deer headed for shelter. More shots, and more deer, all of them at a distance.

The trip across to the foot of the Butte had only taken 15 minutes, but the sun was breaking over the horizon as we started up one of the many game trails picking their way through the rock. The climb was steep and we were forced to stop a couple of times to give the horses a blow. From our vantage point on the open slope we could see both the hunters and the hunted moving in every direction.

We pushed the horses up the trail as hard as we dared. Our assumed advantage was rapidly passing us by. Still a ways from the top, Lawrence groaned and pointed toward a flash of hunter's orange moving through the trees above us. We had been out-maneuvered!

At this point there was nothing for us to do but finish the climb. The frequency of the gunfire around us was starting to slow, and the last shot we heard came from the direction of the pines on the top of the Butte.

The gunfire had ended, the smoke had cleared, and the sun was full up when we at last reached the woods at the top of Black Butte. The white tail-flashes, which we had seen en mass earlier, were now gone - the deer all brushed up somewhere. We had been skunked!

As we rode along through the trees looking over the country spread around us, my attention was pulled to the ground off to my right. A prime Whitetail buck lay motionless by the trail.

Climbing down from my horse I quickly assessed the animal. It was still warm. Further inspection revealed a bullet hole centered cleanly in the brisket.

Lawrence and I tied up our horses and sat on a nearby log. We sipped our coffee and tried to figure out where we had gone wrong. When we had each finished our second cup, we decided that we had waited long enough. Donning plastic gloves to keep our hands and arms clean, we pulled out our knives and field-dressed the animal.

Inside the deer's chest the damage was massive. A large caliber slug had expanded as it penetrated, destroying the heart and one lung. Mortally wounded deer seldom fall over instantly like the men who are shot in the movies, but this one couldn't have traveled far after being hit. What kind of slob hunter, we wondered, could have walked away and left this buck to die?

There was still no one around when we finished the job, so we heisted the deer up and across my saddle. A few lengths of bale twine secured the critter. From atop his steed Lawrence gave me a hand up behind him; riding double, we led my loaded horse down off the butte.

We made it back to the barn with plenty of morning to spare. There was a pulley set-up in the back shed just for the purpose of hanging such a carcass, and we made use of it now. Rose had fresh coffee and cookies ready for us, and we told her our story as we nibbled and sipped.

We were in the house for coffee the following Saturday when an outfit pulled up in the yard. The driver was familiar to us as the proprietor of a tire shop in Chinook, and he was again seeking permission to hunt. The man laid out his battle plan for the weekend, and told us excitedly about "the one that got away" the week before.

He'd been up on Black Butte last Sunday early, he said, and spotted a nice buck between two trees. He'd gotten off a quick shot, he said; but he missed. The buck had run off.

Lawrence and I sympathized with the fellow, and exchanged knowing glances over our coffee cups. We had already enjoyed the first steaks from that prime alfalfa-fed deer. We saw no reason to spoil the man's day by gloating over *our* success

Fall Sort

The headquarters for the Mitchell Ranch lay 34 miles south of Chinook. There was an oil road to Cleveland, where there was a post office, a bar, and a two-room school. From there it was a hard 7 miles through a rocky canyon to reach the ranch.

At the time I worked for them, the ranch was running 1200 cows. The cows were wintered and calved at the home ranch, and summered on the Fort Belknap Indian reservation. The permanent working facilities at the headquarters would hold only a fourth of cattle, and it was more expedient to do the corral work in whatever field the cattle were at the time. We had a portable corral setup that was transported in a trailer that doubled as a loading chute. With all the panels in a circle, we could corral about 400 pairs. We branded in the portable corrals, and we did the fall pregnancy testing in them. We would also ship out of them.

With 1200 calves to ship in the fall, it would take 10 truckloads to get them all. (A semi hauls around 100 calves, and we kept back some 200 heifers for replacements.) There were only 5 semis hauling cattle in the area, and loading all of them would be a day's work, so we had to be prepared to ship on two different days. Steer calves bring about 5% more per pound, and must be weighed separately. We also needed to cut out the top end of the heifers to save for replacing cows as they got too old to remain in the herd.

The week before we would ship, we brought the entire herd up closer to the headquarters. Five of us were ahorseback: Lawrence Mitchell - in his 60s, Doug Mitchell – in his 30s, Doug's wife Joanne, Doug's brother-in-law Noel, and me. We gathered them into a fence corner and began sorting off the steer calves and their mothers.

We couldn't separate the cows from their calves with a week to go before shipping. The calves would have lost some 25 pounds apiece and would be far more likely to get very sick from the stress of weaning and shipping. Neither could we deal with the whole herd on the day when we would be shipping less than half of them. So we had to separate the 1200 pairs into 3 herds that would be handled on different days. We began with the steer pairs.

With the herd in the corner, each of us ahorseback would study the cattle in front of us looking for a calf to "mother up". As soon as any of us spotted a steer pair, that person would swoop in, cut them off, and start them for the gate. If anyone else had a pair headed out, we might throw ours in with theirs and take a larger group. The remaining riders made sure the herd stayed in the corner.

As a rider pushed more cattle through the gate he would add them to the tally, and as returned to the herd he would holler out the total number we now had out. We worked steadily from soon after daylight until almost dark, and it was into the third day when we had 500 steer pairs cut out – enough to fill the trucks.

The week had started out with nice fall weather – 40° and sunny during the day. By Wednesday, however, the temperature had dropped and snow was falling.

I had been riding my horse Red for the first two days. He was a 4-year-old QH/Arab cross, and an excellent cow horse. I had broke him the previous winter, and used him every day for several months during calving, branding, and trailing. After being out to pasture for the summer, I had ridden him again trailing the cattle home from the reservation. But after two solid days of cutting, Red was tired.

On the third day I gave my horse a rest. Charley was a big tall horse that was used as a spare. When I started out on him I understood why. He was tall enough, and I had on enough clothes, that I had to maneuver him into a low spot to get my foot into the stirrup. His gait riding out to the field was rough and awkward. And when we started cutting out pairs, it was obvious that he had no cow savvy.

By that third day we'd already gotten all the steer pairs that mothered up and handled well. Now we were after the renegades that were hiding among the heifers. They were harder to find and harder to cut out. I was on a horse that didn't understand what we were doing, and didn't have much rein. The weather was colder, the light was poor, and the snow made traveling more difficult. Cowboying was beginning to lose its joy. I was sure glad to head back to the barn later in the afternoon.

It wasn't until I rode a different horse that I realized what a team Red and I had become. Somehow he knew which cow and which calf I was after, even when the pair split up and tried to duck away in the herd. Was Red feeling the subtle movements of my fingers through the reins, the changes in my butt muscles or shifting of my weight? Was he reading the cattle in the same way I was/ Or was he reading my mind?

On the fourth day I saddled Red again. It was great to be back with my partner! We had enough steer pairs to fill the first group of 5 trucks, and now we were sorting off the better heifer pairs that would be kept on the ranch.

The snow was piling up, and footing was becoming a problem for the horses. The snow began to cake up under the shoes, making snowballs that could build up several inches thick. The weather had been nice when we started, and none of the horses had pads under their shoes. I tried spraying "Pam" on the bottom of their feet, but the oil soon wore off and the snow built up again. Without shoes the horses would have no traction.

Noel had an old school bus outfitted as a camping rig. By midweek we pulled it into the field so that we could go inside to take a coffee break and get out of the weather. And it kept on snowing.

At noon on Thursday, Red was dragging again. I took Charley for the afternoon work. By the end of the day I was more tired than the horse - from pulling, turning, and spurring him to do my share in sorting out heifers.

On Friday we were getting toward the end. With 500 steer pairs and 200 heifer pairs out, there were still 500 pairs. We opened another gate so that we could send steer pairs one way and heifer pairs another. The job went faster with the herd trimmed down in size – a fourth the cattle makes it four times easier to match up what's left.

I started out on Red, and rode him until morning coffee. Then I changed to Charley and rode him until noon. Neither Red nor I were having fun when we went back out after dinner, and I swapped horses again mid-afternoon, but we finished the job just at dark.

On Saturday the horses finally got a rest – but not the men. The cold and snow would pull weight off those calves that would cost thousands of dollars. We would have to feed them until shipping day. Another winter had started, and the cycle of ranch life continued.

Mixed up Mamas

Bert and Marie Artz had a beautiful ranch on Elk Creek, out of Augusta. It wasn't as big as some Montana ranches, but it was as efficiently run as any in the state. I had first worked for them when I was fresh out of high school. They are a particular pair, and the training I got there has set the tone for my entire working career.

Bert was a fair man, and he enjoyed a joke as well as anyone. But he was serious about his work, and he expected the same from his employees. His attitude was summarized by his instructions to us when we began haying: "Every morning you check out your machines: check the gas, and oil, and tires; look it over for leaks and loose bolts. **There will be <u>no</u> careless breakdowns.**"

I had worked for him on and off for several years, and the spring of 1974 I helped with calving. Activities of this season were no-nonsense as usual. We had a routine which we followed, insuring that all the cattle received the best of care.

Our first stop of every day was the "outside" bunch of cows. This was the group of cows which were not yet ready to calve. After feeding them, we would work through and look for any which were showing signs of imminent parturition. The ones which were showing to be near term we cut into the "heavy" lot.

The heavies were in a small field which cornered onto the calving shed. This was the field which we would be checking on a regular basis around the clock, for here was where the calves were born. After checking and feeding this bunch, we would spend some time doing chores in the shed.

Calving is a labor-intensive time. Some cows must have assistance in calving. Some calves need help to nurse. There are mix-ups and sickness to deal with, and weather can sometimes threaten the new babies. The shed was bedded well with fresh straw, and there were pens along the side to separate problem pairs.

This big barn was divided in the middle - the heavy cows coming in on one side, the new pairs going out through the other. As each calf became strong enough to travel, the pair was pushed on out into the field with the "outside pairs".

We fed each group as we went, and looked everything over for any signs of trouble. By dinner time we taken care of all four groups of cattle and had refilled our wagon with hay.

As I said, Bert was a fair man. He rarely asked me to work after supper. He and Marie took turns checking the cattle every few hours during the night. After dinner Bert would catch a nap. My afternoon assignment was to ride back out to the cattle and look after things while Bert slept.

I would take care of anyone that needed help calving; pen any pairs that were not doing well; take cold calves into the shed; move out solid pairs; milk out big-teated cows; tie up and suckle cows who wouldn't claim their calves; feed weak calves; rope and doctor scouring calves; and finally, put the heavy cows in the shed at dark.

One morning while we were working in the shed, Bert hollered over to me. "I'm missing a calf over here in the pairs. Have you seen an extra over on your side?"

"No", I replied. "But guess what? We've got a set of twins!"

"Are you sure that my calf didn't get in with that cow?" Bert asked suspiciously.

"I'm sure. I put this cow in the pen after she had the first calf. The second one came after the pair was in the pen."

We spent an hour looking for the missing calf. We walked all around the outside fence looking for tracks of the calf, or of a coyote. We broke ice for a ways along the creek. We looked through the outside pairs for an extra mouth. We finally decided the calf had gone under the ice and on down Elk Creek.

We were in the middle of feeding the outside pairs when I had an embarrassing realization. "Turn this rig around, Bert. I just figured out where your calf went."

I had come out the afternoon before to find a new calf up and sucking. I remembered being surprised that he was already dried off and stable on his feet in the short time I had been gone for dinner. It was now obvious that this calf had crawled through the fence and "grannyed" up to a cow which was soon to bear her own calf.

The "Granny Syndrome" is not uncommon, especially in herds that are managed in confinement as these were. A cow goes all winter without a calf, and she has no interest. But the same hormones that cause the onset of labor also trigger the urge to "mother".

In the short time just before her own calf is born, the cow will be willing to accept any calf which sucks her. Within a few hours of birth, however, the cow and calf mark each other by smell. After that, neither will accept a new pairing without several days of enforced bondage.

Bert didn't really chew on me for my mistake. He just grumbled a little under his breath and made a few snide comments. An episode like this is just another of the challenges that are a part of calving.

Back at the barn we headed for the pen with "twin" calves. After a short debate we selected one of the twins to put with the cow who was bawling for her lost baby.

Reunited in another pen, the cow sniffed the calf anxiously. She seemed to be satisfied that this calf was indeed hers, and soon the calf was sucking at her udder.

It was a week or two later when I walked into the shed and found <u>three</u> calves in a pen with one cow. My heart began to race as I mentally reviewed the circumstances surrounding this cow. Where had I found her, and when? How could I have gotten <u>two</u> extra calves in the pen? I was near panic trying to figure out how I had screwed up, and what I was going to tell Bert.

I hid out in the shed trying to make sense of the situation until Bert called out that he was ready to go.

"I've got a bit of a problem here, Bert."

"What have you done now?" he asked in a condescending tone of voice.

"I've got one cow and three calves."

"#&*<@>" muttered Bert.

So we spent another hour looking through the cows. This time we were looking for a cow (or two) which was missing a calf. But we never came up short of calves, and never found any reason to suspect that these calves weren't all hers. The cow had born triplets!

For a while, we left all three calves on their mother. She was concerned for each of them, and had enough milk for all while they were still so young. But we knew that as the calves grew the competition would leave one or more short-changed.

The easiest way to graft a calf to a new mother is to "jacket" him with the hide of the dead calf and pen them up together. The cow recognizes the scent of her own calf draped over the body of a new live one. When the graft calf gets hungry enough, he begins to suck his new mama. Within a few days the hide can be removed, and the new pair go happily on their way.

We didn't lose many calves that spring, but eventually we found mothers on which to graft the two bonus babies. Each was given his own mama to love him, and provide him his full share of milk.

Spaying Heifers

One day, at his N Lazy A Ranch out of Augusta, Bert sent me to run in the horses. He said that our next project for the day was to spay some heifers.

I was always ready to work cattle, and yearlings are the most fun to work. They are usually full of sass and vinegar, and will give a cowboy and his horse some sport. We threw on our saddles, called the dogs, and headed out toward a field alongside Haystack Butte.

This was a fantastic day, the kind a cowboy lives for. It was late in May with blue skies and green grass. The day in and day out grind of feeding and calving were done, and the long days of haying hadn't started. The scenery along the Front Range of the Rocky Mountains is absolutely the best there is.

It was maybe 4 miles to the field where the heifers were pastured, and of course we kicked the horses into a trot. Most cow horses aren't bred for a fancy gait; they only walk, trot, and gallop. A trot is sure not the smoothest gait in the world, but it eats up the country. A horse can jog all day without getting used up, and still have the reserve to bust out when necessary to turn the cattle.

Most cowmen save back the best half of their heifer calves every year to replace cows that are getting too old to winter well. In the spring, this bunch of replacements are sorted again to pick out the best heifers. We had plenty of grass and would summer them all, but Bert didn't want the poorer ones bred - they would be sold for beef in the fall.

The value of these heifers would be limited as beef animals, however, if they were to get bred during the summer. And it would be nearly impossible to maintain their maidenhood on the range. So we would spay these heifers before we turned out the bulls, and thus be guaranteed that they would not be carrying a calf at sale time.

These yearlings were in a field with a bunch of cows and calves, and our first job was to cut out the ones we wanted to take back to the corrals. Because we had two such distinct classes of livestock, the cattle neatly separated themselves. As we rode through the gate with our dogs, the cows all threw up their heads and bellered for their calves.

Dogs can be a liability among small calves, and it takes a good cow dog to stand up to a cow's challenge. One on one, a quiet and aggressive dog can hold his own. One bark, however, will bring on the whole herd and put the run on the best of dogs.

There was a mad scramble as the mamas and babies ran around bawling and sniffing each other to make a positive identification. The dogs stayed close at our heels and kept an eye over their shoulders on the alert for attacking cows.

The cows and calves were allowed to split off as they paired up, and the unhampered yearlings quickly moved toward the front of the herd. We slowly worked up through the bunch, sifting the yearlings out into the lead. It wasn't long before we had a clean bunch of heifers out the gate and headed back toward headquarters.

The trip back to the corrals was fast and fun. As soon as the yearlings realized their situation, they kicked up their heels and ran. They weren't really running <u>from</u> anything, and they certainly weren't running <u>to</u> anything. These yearlings were just running for the fun of it. And we followed along, keeping them headed in the right general direction.

It really got western when we aimed them toward the corrals. Yearlings can be pretty ignorant. They seemed never to have seen a bridge before. They passed the gate three times at a high lope without ever seeing the hole. When they finally did look into the corrals, the heifers saw boogers and spooks in the shadows, and they broke and ran again.

My horse and I were having a fine time! He was quite a cutting horse, and he enjoyed the game as much as I. But gradually the heifers wore down. Their breaks got slower and their runs got shorter. Finally one of the yearlings sniffed her way through the gate, and the others crowded in behind her.

The fun ended when we slammed the gate behind them. We climbed down, tied up the horses, and started to work. The sorting would now be all done afoot.

As we stood in the corral, Bert eyeballed the heifers. His potential profits would depend in part on how well he chose his future cow herd from among these prospects. We spent the rest of the morning sorting off the "keeper" heifers into a separate pen.

The veterinarian, Bill Patton, arrived just before dinner. Cow-country vets cover a vast area where McDonald's is not available, and Bill was a welcome addition to our table. We ate, visited, and rested awhile before we headed back to the corrals.

In order to restrain cattle for such things as branding and vaccinating, every ranch has a chute. This is a long narrow alley constructed of poles or planks, through which a line of cattle can pass single file. At the end is a steel headgate and squeeze to catch and control each individual. As we loaded the chute corral with cattle, Bill set up by the headgate.

The job of keeping the chute full is a hard and dirty job. A man is crowded in a small pen with a bunch of scared and confused cattle who don't want to be there. The corrals, cattle, and ground are covered with a foul-smelling, semi-liquid material, which a few hours ago was "just grass and water". According to the unwritten "Code of the West," this job falls to the person of least seniority, and today I was that person.

As I moved cattle into the chute, someone on the outside would shove a pole in behind them to keep the yearlings from backing out. I was kept busy filling the chute and was surprised at how fast the cattle were moving through.

Castrating bull-calves is a quick job; spaying heifers is a lot more complicated. Yet each of these girls was only in the chute about a minute. I'd never seen the procedure done, but I knew it required surgery. The speed of the operation convinced me that I'd misunderstood what was to be done to these heifers today.

For most of an hour I was kept busy working cattle into the chute. I'd only had a few chances to hang over the fence to see what the other men were doing. When I finally had the last of the heifers in the chute, I climbed over to watch the operation.

When they were ready for the next animal, Bert would open the gate at the back of the squeeze. Seeing an opening, a heifer would charge through toward the wide open spaces. But Dick was on the headgate, and he never missed. With a crash, he slammed the gate closed just ahead of her shoulders while Bert drew up the sides to hold her tight.

The process of spaying each heifer was amazingly quick and efficient. So fast did it happen that I used my watch to time it. The whole operation took 45 seconds - less time than it takes to tell it.

In his right hand, Dr. Patton held the tool to make the incision. It was a metal A-frame affair made of surgical steel. The legs of the tool were about 14 inches long, hinged at the apex. The base of the triangle was curved outward, and through that curve protruded a scalpel blade, affixed to the end of one of the legs.

With the heifer immobilized in the squeeze, the vet would press that curve against the skin of the heifer's flank, puncturing her hide with the scalpel blade. A quick squeeze of the legs of the tool drew the blade along the arc of the base, leaving a neat and perfect incision.

Reaching in with his left hand to grasp the heifer's ovaries, Bill exchanged the A-frame scalpel in his right hand for the long-handled spaying shears. The shears were inserted along his arm into the yearling's abdomen. A quick snip, and the vet withdrew the severed ovaries with his left hand, dropping them into a bucket.

When Bill's left hand returned to the heifer, it bore a measure of antibiotic powder which he tossed into the open incision. Next swinging to the right, he exchanged the shears for a hog ring pliers. Three quick clips and the incision was closed.

It took only three-quarters of an hour through the chute to do the whole job. Including all of the delays between heifers, we averaged one and a half minutes apiece from start to finish! The cost that year was $3/head, and we spayed 30 heifers; the doc had earned $90 in less than an hour.

In comparison to my wage of $450 per month, the doc's pay was outrageous. But considering his obvious expertise and efficiency, Doctor Patton was worth every penny.

Cow Pony

Like me, Arty is a Jack of all trades. And like me, he takes every job seriously. Whether he is trucking, logging, or cowboying, he puts his heart into the job. Consequently, he always maintains the proper equipment for each task.

When it came time for the cowboying part of the business, Arty was well mounted. He had only five horses, but they were as good a string as a guy could want. Of course every horse has a different disposition and different physical characteristics, and these differences make each individual more suited for a different horseback job.

Old Lester had been Arty's top horse for a number of years. He'd bought the horse from Les Canfield up in that Dearborn country. Les was a big black horse who had seen and done it all. He was quiet, steady, and smart. But he was old and crippled, and had been relegated to the job of kids horse.

Racehorse was a half Thoroughbred mare who could really cover the country. She was great if you had someplace to go, but she wasn't as good at turning a cow.

Willy was a good stout horse who was kind of "boogery". He had both stamina and agility, and was as good an all-round horse as a guy could want, if the guy was cowboy enough to stay with him.

Rocket was a teenaged buckskin of medium height. He was the smartest of the bunch, and the laziest. Rocket had a rather short stride which didn't keep up with the other horses too well at a walk, but Rocket was quick, and he knew cows!

Arty had only had 150 cows, so calving was an easy one-man operation. He was spending most of his time on the road with the truck and left me home to care for the cows.

Diarrhea - known to the cowman as "scours" - is a common ailment among the young calves. One of my daily chores was to doctor whatever calves were showing signs of sickness. They must each be caught and given antibiotic boluses for a series of at least three days.

In an open field, the most efficient way to catch these calves is to ride through on a good horse and rope each one. After he is given his pills, the calf is marked with a grease stick to distinguish who has been given what, when. Before Arty left on another road trip he gave me instructions to use Rocket for the job.

That first spring, I hadn't yet gotten to know these horses well. I had ridden Racehorse some, and liked her fiery disposition. Rocket was getting up in years, and mostly the kids had been riding him. I wasn't sure why Arty insisted I ride the lazy old plug, and I wasn't happy about it.

But, I followed instructions and saddled Rocket when it came time to rope calves.

As I say, he was short-strided and lazy. We rode through the cattle, gave chase to a few, and caught fewer. He just didn't seem to have the speed or ambition to put me up in a position to rope those calves.

When Arty returned home with the truck, I complained. But he just couldn't understand my trouble. Rocket had been Arty's calf roping horse in College Rodeo, and he knew the horse had the ability. It was obvious that Arty had more faith in the horse than he had in me. The instructions stood.

By the next week, my aim with the lariat had improved a bit – I caught the first calf with my first loop. Rocket seemed to take note of that, and he gave a little more effort on the second calf – I caught that one with my first loop also! When the third calf broke away from the herd Rocket put me right up on him where it would be hard to miss!

Before long, the horse and I were making quite a team at this calf-roping job. It was then that I began to appreciate the horse, lazy and all, and to understand his initial reluctance to exert himself.

Rocket liked to rope as much as I did. And as long as we was roping, he would give it his all to put me up for the shot. But as far as he could see, I had been just throwing my rope on the ground; Rocket was too lazy and too wise to waste a lot of energy on that.

Over time, I learned that it was Rocket's laziness that made him an outstanding cow pony. He understood that a little extra effort to get his rider quickly in good position for a throw at the critter would actually save a lot of effort in chasing the animal around and around before finally connecting with the loop.

And likewise, extra effort to turn a cow in the gate now would save a long chase to bring her back.

As it took a while for me to bring my *roping* skill up to par with Rocket, likewise it took awhile for me to keep up with his cutting ability. The first time he whirled to turn a cow, I was so far behind him that I ended up on the ground. It took months of riding Rocket to develop my balance to a level that I no longer *hindered* him at doing his job.

Any time a cowboy has a choice of horses to do a particular job, he selects the one most suited to the work at hand. As long as I worked on Arty's place on Flat Creek I had a choice. For the long rides to cover country looking for cattle, Racehorse was my pick. If there was anything big to rope, I wanted Willy.

But if it was a matter of roping calves or cutting cattle, that lazy old bastard Rocket would be my mount.

Double Clutching

Augusta Montana is a small town - in 1976 there were fewer than 500 people living there. The community sits beside the South Fork of the Sun River on rolling short-grass prairie in the shadows of the East Slope of the Rockies. The surrounding area is primarily cow country, but the nearby foothills provide other opportunities also. There is some logging, there are tourists, and there is HUNTING.

The area abounds in game: fish, duck, geese, deer, antelope, bear, cougar, pheasant, and grouse. Just over the Divide from Augusta lays the Bob Marshall Wilderness. Numerous pack-trails lead off from the ends of the roads and back into time. Motorized traffic is not allowed in the wilderness, and a large number of horses and mules are used to pack in the hunters and equipment.

In the fall, a significant percentage of the area population is involved in the outfitting industry, providing services for the many out-of-state hunters looking for a chance to spend some time in the rugged outdoors, hoping to bag a huge bull elk.

Four-wheel-drive pickups line the main street, large-bore rifles evident in their rear windows. Bearded men sporting hunter's orange clothing line up in the local establishments to buy hunting licenses, ammunition, and supplies. Large quantities of "antifreeze", "snake-bite remedy", and "cold medicine" are marketed in the name of trusted medicine men with names like Jim Beam and Jack Daniels.

A sister city to Augusta is Lincoln, Montana - southwest of Augusta, 55 miles by the highway. Lincoln lies just to the west of Rogers Pass, and 100 miles south of Marias Pass in Glacier Park. These two passes mark the northern and southern borders of the Bob Marshall Wilderness.

Lincoln and Augusta are connected by several features: their relative proximity (by Montana standards), their mutual involvement in the hunting business, and a shared high school.

In the seventies Lincoln was a sleepy little village with a smaller year-round population than Augusta. There were only a few dozen high school youth - not enough to justify their own facility. A school bus left Lincoln every morning in the dark to take its load over the pass and out on the prairie to the High School at Augusta.

Some of the kids slept on the 2-hour trip. Others studied or socialized. To be involved in extra-curricular activities, however, a student from Lincoln usually boarded out with a family in Augusta and went home only on the weekend. This boarding arrangement strengthened the ties between the two communities by growing a bond between the families involved in the boarding arrangement.

In 1976 my brother Mark and I each worked the fall hunt as guides. We both lived in Augusta, but our employment took us over the Divide to trailheads out of Lincoln. We made the trip from Augusta together in Mark's 1956 Chevy pickup.

After the first hunt was over, Mark and I climbed into his pickup for the trip home. We had spent the last 10 days in the wilderness with a bunch of smelly men, and we were eager to return home to our families and our showers. We headed up the highway with considerably more speed and comfort than we had on the horses we'd been riding. But as the road led higher toward Rogers Pass, the engine began turning faster and the pickup began losing speed.

It was quickly evident that the clutch was the culprit. Mark had noted weeks before that its grip was becoming weaker with each trip, and had hoped he could get by until he had both the time and money to make the repair.

Mark and I leaned forward, urging the pickup on - but the wheels didn't respond. Mark shifted down to second; the smell of burning clutch wafted up through the cab. Finally he spotted a side-road and nosed the pickup off the highway. We were still 40 miles from home and the pickup would go no further.

We weren't long by the road before a passing motorist offered us a ride. Even yet in Montana people are quick to offer help to motorists in trouble along the expanses of empty highway. We were home by dark.

The next day we took my outfit - a Toyota Land Cruiser - and headed back up the mountain. We had *heard* of the Automobile Club, but we weren't members. The cost of a tow-truck was definitely not in the budget.

We found the pickup exactly as we left it. With a tow-chain we pulled it back onto the highway and resumed our trek toward Augusta.

The Land Cruiser was no power house, but we were making good time toward the summit in second gear. I figured I had enough momentum to make third. Tow-ropes with their elastic properties had not yet become common, and any slack in the chain would be pulled up with a jerk when I accelerated. To minimize the effect I did a speed shift, jamming into the next gear with barely a pause.

But my clutch-work was too quick and the gear change resulted in a distinct bang. Suddenly *my* engine was turning free, with no connection to the drive shaft. I had just blown my clutch also!

Still chained together, both rigs drifted to a halt. Mark and I sat in the pickup cab and discussed our options. The engine in Mark's Chevy was a transplant, and he didn't know what size replacement clutch he needed. The Toyota was foreign made, and parts would have to come from Great Falls. We each owned one vehicle, and each of those vehicles sat near the highway west of the Divide in a pile of snow. We were plumb afoot.

Finally Mark scratched his head and said "I don't know about you, but I have tools enough to pull my clutch here."

I inventoried the job in my mind: a seven-sixteenths wrench to pull the bolts from the flywheel cover; half inch wrench to remove the four nuts from the universal joint; a three-quarter inch wrench to pull the four bolts holding the transmission to the bell housing; then a nine-sixteenths wrench for the six bolts holding on the clutch. We were both Chevy men from way back, and had we each done the job several times before.

Mark opened his tool box and pulled out a tarp to spread on the snow under the pickup. Grabbing the four wrenches and a pry bar he crawled underneath and went to work.

My brother was cold, wet and short-tempered when he emerged a half hour later, but the worn out clutch was in his hand.

Again we hitched a ride to Augusta with little lost time. The driver deposited us in front of Kreb's Service where we could begin our search for a replacement clutch.

It was no trouble to locate the proper parts, and the mechanic even loaned us a spline to align them to the transmission once they were in place. The next morning we were back on the road with our thumbs in the air.

Reinstalling the clutch wasn't a big job, and would have been quickly and easily done with the pickup on a hoist in a heated garage. But we were working in the great out of doors, under the "Big Sky", in the Rocky Mountains in the fall, and snow was spitting out of the grey sky. The cold metal rapidly drew the life out of our fingers as we worked. To warm up, I shoveled tracks through the snow from the pickup back on to the highway.

There was adequate incentive to move quickly at our work, and we were soon ready to roll. Once the pickup was again headed up the road we hooked the chain to the Land Cruiser and tried the pass for a third time in twenty-four hours.

Back in Augusta we had to get ready for another hunt. We'd been out of camp for two days and would be heading back in the next morning. I called the dealer in Great Falls to order a clutch for my rig before I left for another ten days in the wilderness.

After the hunt when my chance finally came to repair the Land Cruiser clutch, I wasn't sure what the job would entail. There was nothing to do but crawl underneath and look things over.

The u-joint looked identical to Mark's Chevy. It was metric, so the half inch wrench wouldn't fit, but a twelve millimeter did the job. There were the same four bolts holding on the transmission, and again the size was the metric equivalent to the Chevrolet set-up. I was soon able to slide out from underneath with the unit sitting on my chest.

Going back after the clutch, I grabbed a metric wrench that looked close to nine-sixteenths. There were the same six bolts holding on the pressure plate, and the wrench fit!

Aligning a new clutch disc is almost impossible without a proper tool. Mark had used a spline borrowed at the local garage. A Chevy spline is very common, but where would I find one for a Toyota? Everything else on the Land Cruiser looked identical - maybe the input shaft would be too.

Sure enough, the spline fit! The metric measurement was a hair bigger so the shaft was a bit sloppy in the hole, but it was close enough to accomplish the purpose. Within an hour the job was done.

My first experience with a six cylinder Chevy had been a 1938 pickup. That Toyota engine, built 31 years later, was almost identical - the Japanese had been wise enough to use a tried and true design copied directly from General Motors. The only significant difference between the two engines, built three decades and two continents apart, was a measurement in millimeters rather than inches.

Mule String

I would never be considered a true "packer" by those who practice that trade on a full-time basis, but I got a pretty good introduction into the art over the course of several seasons shoeing and guiding for the V-A Ranch out of Lincoln, Montana. This outfit ran some 30 head each of horses and mules, using them for summer trips and fall hunts into the Bob Marshal Wilderness.

Most people know that a mule is the offspring of a <u>Jack</u> - a male donkey - and <u>mare</u> – a female horse. And most folks have heard some reference to a mule's character, such as the saying: "stubborn as a mule". While a mule is genetically half horse, he is all mule – and that's a whole 'nother animal.

Maybe half of all the pack animals in the west are horses. But if a guy is serious about moving the most freight with the least work and upkeep he will choose a mule. Mules are smaller than horses – both in height and width – yet they carry more, eat less, live longer, and keep themselves out of trouble far better. Their feet are much smaller than those of a horse, yet they have thicker walls that withstand the trail better than those of a horse.

Not everyone appreciates mules. Their big drawback is their disposition: mules are smarter than horses – and they are more independent. It is said that if you ever abuse a mule he will get you – eventually. It is also said that in order to get along with a mule you have to be smarter than *he* is.

I got acquainted with all of the mules at the V-A Ranch while I was shoeing them. And maybe more important, they got acquainted with me. My education continued when the time came to hit the trail into hunting camp.

Each mule has a personality, and mule personalities tend to be both more varied and more distinct than those of horses. As different horses are better suited to roping, or cutting, or traveling, or taking care of kids, different mules are better for different types of loads and different positions in the string. As we began lashing gear onto the mules for my first experience at packing, Phil was giving me directions as to the order in which to load them and the type and size of their pack.

The horses and mules were all saddled while tied to the hitching rails. Then the food and gear was distributed among the "mantie" tarps spread on the ground. (Manties – from the Spanish "mantilla", which means 'covering'.) Each tarp was then wrapped around the pile of gear and trussed up like a Christmas present with a mantie-rope. These mantied loads were then paired up according to size and weight.

First to be packed were the lead mules. Each of us had a mule that led easily, stood quietly, and wouldn't be bothered by any of the activity along the trail. The cinch was drawn up and a pack was tied on each side of the mule with the sling-rope attached to the packsaddle. As each successive mule was loaded, his lead-rope was tied to the rigging of the last mule to be packed, adding him to the string.

Mules who were buddies in the pasture were tied together in line; especially quiet mules were given the eggs; mules that might buck were put at the tail end where they wouldn't stir up a ruckus behind them.

As each string grew in length it took on a life of its own, and began to writhe like a snake. When any mule changed position for any reason, all the mules behind him would re-adjust. The mule on the tail end was continually being whipped from one side to another as any one of the mules ahead of him turned to look at something different.

When all the mules were packed, the dudes were helped to secure their coats and rifles, and mount up. The riders started up the trail for camp, and we mule-skinners climbed on our horses.

Swinging into the saddle while holding the lead-rope takes a bit of coordination. One must position his horse on his left side, perpendicular to the lead-mule on the right side. Then holding his reins in his left hand while grabbing the horn, he must hold the lead-rope in the right hand while positioning his stirrup, and swing his right leg up <u>under</u> the lead-rope and over the cantle.

When he is sitting tight and ready to go he shouts a "Heads Up!" to his mules, and starts down the trail. Each mule watches the animal in front of him and begins to walk before his lead-rope pulls tight.

A good packer looks back over his string frequently at first to see that all the packs are riding even. A mile or so up the trail we stop to go down the line checking cinches and loads to be sure everything is tight and level.

For the most part the mules just follow their leader quietly down the trail. But there are various obstacles to be negotiated on even the best-maintained of trails: creeks, switchbacks, tree limbs, and pack-strings headed in the opposite direction.

The stride of any animal shortens when he is going downhill, and lengthens going up. As the lead slows going downhill, the string begins to compress like an accordion. Each animal may hesitate a half second in crossing a creek, then pick up stride going up the other side. A good packer holds up his horse to allow the entire string to cross the creek before allowing him to stride out again. Soon enough the string will be stretched out as they get back into their traveling pace.

A careless packer may allow his horse to step out immediately across the creek, quickly stretching out the lead-rope from the mule who is just now hesitating a bit before stepping across. When that mule strides out to follow the lead-rope it tightens the rope behind him. In a long string, the lead-mule might have had two feet of slack to negotiate the creek. But he is now hurrying to catch up to the horse that is already striding out, leaving only one foot of slack to the second mule. The horse and the first two mules are already stepping out when the third mule gets to the creek with no slack left, and he must hurry right through with no hesitation. The fourth mule is still coming downhill in a shortened stride when the slack is all gone, and now he must hurry on down-slope and across the creek to keep up with the leaders.

The front half of the string is now striding out with their lead-ropes pulled taut while the back half is still bunched up coming downhill. Eventually the strain is too much: a pig-tail snaps and the pack-string breaks in two.

The "pig-tail" is a short piece of light rope tied into the ring at the end of a pair of straps coming from the back of a packsaddle. The lead-rope to the next animal is tied to this pig-tail, which acts as a kind of a fuse - breaking apart before more permanent damage occurs. A packer usually has several spares in his saddle bags.

The pig-tail is at risk again when the string is going around a switch-back in the trail. The horse slows up to make the turn, and then he's ready to step out again after he negotiates the bend. If the packer isn't looking out for all the animals behind him, part of the string can be pulled across short of the corner. Again the accordion effect: the lead slows to make the corner and the string compresses. The lead steps out and the sting stretches as the mules further back are just now coming to the corner

Meeting another string is one of the challenges of leading a pack-train – somebody has to pull off the trail. The loaded string has the right of way, and a shorter string will likely defer to a longer one – I've seen some strings of 16 head in a line. Seldom are the meetings in an open place. They usually occur somewhere in the thick of the woods, and one string must thread itself around through the trees while the other goes by on the trail.

The path through the trees can be quite convoluted, searching for openings wide enough for packs jutting out on both sides. Mules are pretty savvy about how much clearance they need for their load, and some may have a pack that is too bulky for the terrain. Or a mule might be gawking over at the other string, or at the leader who is circling back around to find a hole through the trees, and he may put his head on the wrong side of a tree. Again the pigtail breaks and the packer must stop to make repairs, then extricate his string from the tangle.

Elk thistles are a common sight in the wilderness. This variety has a tall stalk with a single purple flower on top, and mules find these to be quite compelling. When a mule spots an elk thistle along the trail he will move in close to the animal ahead of him to get as much slack in his lead-rope as possible, then lunge out to bite off the flower as he goes by.

The trip into our Middle Fork Creek camp was about 12 miles, and took all of 4 hours on the trail. One always hopes for a quick, eventless trip.

But four hours of sitting in the saddle was always more than enough for me. I actually *preferred* having some kind of wreck along the way, to break the monotony – in the same way that I almost look forward to a break-down during haying.

And I always had a measure of empathy for the dudes on those trips into the wilderness. My life was centered around horses year round, and riding was part of my job description. But my normal mode of riding was often at a long trot with occasional bursts of loping or running, and my weight was more often on my legs than on my ass. Those four hours at a walk on the trail made _my_ butt tired. What must it feel like to those dudes who rode only once a year?

When the string arrives in camp, the guests are immediately shown to their tent. The lead-mule is tied to the hitching post; the last mule in line is separated from the string, led as close to his destination area as possible, and his packs are dropped to the ground. When all the mules are unloaded, their saddles are removed, they are given a bait of grain, and turned out to pasture in a meadow above camp where they can roll on the ground until the feeling of the saddle is gone, and then trot off to fill their bellies with the lush mountain grass.

The wranglers, however, have yet to unsaddle all the horses and take care of the gear, feed them, open all the packs and distribute their contents, and maybe cut some firewood, before _they_ can sit down to enjoy _their_ apéritif.

It's a tough job, but someone has to do it!

Manhattan

Every hunting trip to the Bob Marshall Wilderness begins the same: men and livestock converge at the trailhead and begin saddling horses and packing mules. The air is crisp, scented with pine, and electric with excitement. The hunters are at last embarking on the adventure that has been growing in their minds for months, and even the veteran packers, guides, and outfitter are eager to get on the trail.

This trip started like all the others, as we began trussing up all the duffle into mantie-loads.

Mantie" is another of the Americanized words that comes to us from Mexico. Mantilla is Spanish for 'cover'. Mantie refers to a tarp that is some eight feet square into which gear is bound up with rope into a package – just like a Christmas present – to sling on the pack saddle.

Booze seems to be an essential supply in every hunting camp, and as usual, I announced to the dudes that they should lay their bottles out so that we could pack them up securely and load them on an appropriate mule. But in this case no one responded. As we were divvying the gear out among the various mantie-tarps I noticed that some of the duffle was a little heavier than usual, and some of the bags had a suspicious gurgle. But *everyone* has a little liquor in the hills and I didn't really pay much attention.

The initial indication of something unusual was at the first stop along the trail to check cinches and re-balance loads. Going down the line of mules I noticed a wet spot in the mantie-tarp under the sling-rope that held the load to the mule. I sniffed the pack, and recognized the odor of beer.

I had warned them, I thought, yet someone had left a six-pack in the top their duffle. Now their gear would be saturated by the leakage. The quantity of liquor that had been hidden away in the luggage didn't become evident until evening.

It was just getting dark when I went into the dude tent to light the lantern. As my eyes adjusted to the dim illumination I glanced around the tent in wonder. There lining the canvass walls were six <u>cases</u> of beer, two <u>cases</u> of brandy, and one <u>case</u> of vermouth. Before I could really comprehend what I was seeing, someone handed me a glass and said "Here, have a Manhattan".

"What in the hell is a Manhattan?" I asked as I tasted the brew.

"Brandy and vermouth," was the reply.

I sampled the drink, and it went down pretty well. I didn't have much time to visit with our guests before someone handed me a fresh glass and said "Here, have another."

When I got up to leave, someone stuck a third glass in my hand. I tried to demur, but the fellow pointed out that the drink was already poured and that it would be a shame to waste it.

Before long these cosmopolitan fellows from back East were educating this Montana hick about the finer points of drinking. They explained that they had two kinds of brandy: one for sipping and one for mixing – and they gave me shots of each so that I could appreciate the subtle differences between the two. I was feeling a little light on the feet when the cook hollered that supper was ready.

It had been a long day, I was hungry, and the food was good. But I was still a little unsteady after filling my belly with steak & potatoes & pie. The visiting around the table in the cook-tent went on for a couple hours before everyone drifted off to beds in their own tents.

My mind hadn't cleared much by the time I crawled into my sack, and my stomach was still feeling a little queasy. When the lantern was shut off the tent began to spin.

Clothed only in my union suit, I crawled to the door and stuck my head out through the tent flap. Thankfully, the stars remained anchored in the sky.

I lay there with my head out in the clear cold night until my body began to shiver. The tent stayed still now as I crawled back into my down sleeping bag, and I was finally able to doze off.

Morning always comes early in the mountains. The days are short to begin with, and it takes a long time for the sun to climb over the Continental Divide and out of the shadows of the trees. *Everyone* had a little to drink the night before, and no one has sympathy for a fellow who feels a little under the weather. There are horses to be run in from night pasture and saddled, mules to be penned up for the day, and then a hearty breakfast before heading out into the dawn for the day's hunt.

Another 25 years passed before I drank a Manhattan again – and that's a whole 'nother story.

Air Rescue!

One of the requirements for an outfitter's license is a current first aid and CPR card. So we all looked to the boss - Gene Youderian - when one of the hunters fell off his stool, unconscious.

It was after supper on the first night in camp, 12 miles from the trailhead into the Bob Marshall Wilderness, with a new bunch of dudes from Minnesota. We'd all filled up on roast beef and gravy, followed that with pie, and washed it all down with lots of strong coffee. Most of us had had a nip or two from one of the bottles on the table, and some of the men were smoking.

Jim was a big man - close to three hundred pounds. From his perch on a stump at the end of the table he had been an active participant in the supper conversation. But with no warning, he had silently toppled over onto the floor.

Before anyone had time to act to his aid, Jim's eyes began to flutter, then they opened. Looking up at the faces above him, he asked "Is it time to get up?"

A hunting camp in the Bob Marshal Wilderness is a very inconvenient place for a medical emergency, and the relief was palpable as the huge form got up off the floor and resumed his seat on the log. But none of us really knew what had caused the sudden loss of consciousness, and there was no way to know when it might happen again.

After a brief discussion it was decided that one of the guides would ride out to summon a helicopter. Even had cell phones been available at that time, coverage is sporadic in the wilderness areas. We caught up a fresh horse and gave him a bait of oats as we threw on the saddle by the light of a lantern.

Bill was given a good flashlight and some last-minute instructions before being sent out into the night.

With a fresh pot of coffee on the stove, the rest of us sat down to wait. There was a subdued conversation at one end of the table, and a cribbage game at the other. Slowly the cook-tent emptied as each person's worry was overcome by sleepiness. The last man turned in after being assured that our "patient' would live through the night.

Breakfast was at its usual time, well before daylight. Everyone was relieved to find that Jim was still alive and well. Our concern for his health was masked by good-natured joking among the men. "When smaller men die up here," we told him, "we just sling them over a log until they freeze. Then they fit on the back of a mule so we can pack them out." But we all kept an ear cocked for the sound of a helicopter.

We hadn't really expected the chopper to arrive in the dark, as there would be no way to locate our camp. There was also some speculation as to source of a "bird", and its point of departure, as this was in the years before medical helicopters were common in regional hospitals of Montana. After the sun was full up, we began listening in earnest for the beat of rotors.

As the morning drug by with no sign of help from the sky, some of the hunters began to grumble. Jim seemed to be in no danger, but what if this had been an emergency? It was 14 hours since the guide had left camp. Could something have happened to *him* in the dark?

It was nearly noon when we finally heard a drone in the distance. The silence of the wilds was shredded as a big military helicopter circled, then put down in the meadow. With the blades still turning, the door opened and out jumped our guide followed by an Air Force medic.

After a quick examination by the medic, Jim followed him out to the bird. The engine sped up, the chopper lifted off, and peace returned to wilderness as it sped off over the trees. With Jim now in good hands, we all clustered around the guide to hear his story.

The ride through the dark had been uneventful. The trail was wide and well kept. Both the Bill and his horse knew it well. The first problem had come when he reached the pickup at 2 AM. The keys had been tucked up under a bumper when we left it near the corrals, but had been knocked to the ground in the dark.

After scratching around in the duff for awhile, Bill had finally found the keys and headed the pickup for the nearest town, Lincoln. When he arrived there, even the bars were closed; so he drove on out to the home ranch and got Gene's wife Martha out of bed.

The two of them had been on the phone for several hours before giving up in disgust - it was impossible at that hour to locate the bigwigs necessary for the authorization of a helicopter and a flight into a designated wilderness.

At 8 AM Bill and Martha had again hit the phones. Permission was received, orders were given, and a helicopter was finally dispatched from Malmstrom Air Force Base nearly a hundred miles away. The chopper then had to fly to Lincoln and pick up Bill to guide them in to our camp.

It turned out that Jim had suffered from cancer a few years back and had a lung removed. His decreased breathing capacity and the high altitude of the hunting camp had left Jim's brain with too little oxygen to function.

The experience left the hunters a little shaken. They had come from an environment where an ambulance was available to their doors in a matter of minutes any time of the day or night.

They had been shown first hand just one of the drawbacks of getting "out of the rat race" and getting "back to nature".

Wool Underwear

Montana can be a rather chilly place, and a cowboy spends his life outside in the elements. For many years, wool underwear was an integral part of my clothing from October through March.

Any time I mention wool underwear, folks respond with "doesn't that itch?" and they never quite believe that I could wear wool next to my skin. But I always bought light-weight, high-quality union suits that were as soft as any other knit.

I generally bought a new pair or two every year, and they were easily available from the Penny's or Sears catalogues. The cost was about $29.95 when wages were $350 a month.

The light union suits laid nicely under the Wrangler jeans and plaid denim shirts that I wore year-round, and kept me comfortable in temperatures another 20-30° colder than the denim clothes alone. For riding a horse or tractor at temperatures below zero I kept a heavy wool union suit that I covered with a wool shirt and pants. That suit was a little courser wool, and it <u>did</u> itch if I would happen to work up a sweat.

The cowboy life is pretty active – slinging bales, roping calves, fixing fence – and the wool underwear did not impair movement. A fellow *did* have to be careful to peel off his jacket before he got too energetic, to prevent sweating.

Wool is an excellent insulator, and is one of the few materials that hold in the heat nearly as well when wet. It wicks the moisture away from the body so you never feel clammy like you can in cotton underwear. I had a dramatic demonstration of its wicking capacity one fall in the mountains.

When we went into a wilderness hunting camp, most trips were scheduled for 10 days. Fall in the mountains is usually chilly,

71

with temperatures below freezing nearly every night. There are no bathroom facilities in a tent-camp in the Bob Marshall Wilderness, so no one takes a shower. The weather was seldom warm enough to encourage a spit bath.

At night, I generally peeled down to my wool union suit before crawling into my sleeping bag. My shirt and jeans accumulated a lot of dust and grime during the day, and I didn't want to take all that filth into my down sleeping bag with me.

Getting in the bag was relatively painless – we usually had a fire going in a corner of the tent. By morning, however, the cold was settled right in. It took an intense concentration of will to climb out of a nice warm sleeping bag into the frosty air of the tent. A fellow had generally worked up a pretty good shiver by the time he was dressed.

Fortunately for us guides, the cook was the first one up. He had a fire going and a fresh pot of coffee before he called us. We had a chance to work off our chill in the cook-tent before going out to wrangle horses in the dark. But back to the underwear...

Because it is usually pretty cold in the mountains at night, and *always* cold in the morning, a fellow is only able to strip down so far and still survive. I might change my outerwear once during the trip, but I usually kept that wool union suit on 24 hours a day for 10 days straight.

I don't know what those hunting camps might smell like to a young lady fresh out of a shower, but I suspect they get pretty rank by the end of a 10-day hunt. We were a bunch of guys, however, and *none* of us smelled any better than the rest.

Maybe that particular smell receptor burns out for a while. Even after wallowing in his own unwashed stench for a week, a hunter can still pick out the musky smell of elk that are close by. I had never given my odor any thought until one particular day when I was cleaning up after returning home from a trip to the mountains.

I had peeled off my dirty clothes on the way to the shower, and left them lying on the washing machine. After enjoying the luxury of clean surroundings and a hot shower until the water heater was empty, I passed my pile of clothes as I left the bathroom.

The steamy air must have cleaned out my nostrils, because I was suddenly hit by the odor of sour sweat emanating from the pile of clothes on the washer.

For some reason I picked up the wool union suit and noticed that it did not carry the same stench as the cotton outerwear. Making a careful comparison, I noted that the cotton shirt had collected most of the smell. As the odor had originated from *within* the clothes, it was obvious that it had wicked through the wool and been absorbed by the cotton.

Likewise, body *moisture* wicks through wool and away from the body – a fact that I also appreciated about wool socks and gloves. Wool socks don't become saturated with sweat and scald the foot like cotton socks do. And wool has the added advantage of maintaining its loft and insulation capacity even while still wet, rather than compressing like down or becoming clammy like cotton.

Insulated bib overalls became available around 1980. Those bibs provide more insulation than wool underwear, and have more capacity for adapting to temperature conditions. You can take off your coat, and your vest, then your bibs as your body temperature or the air temperature rise. And they have the added benefit of keeping your first layer of clothing clean and dry.

In later years I have come to rely on bibs almost exclusively. But they do add a layer of bulk that can be pretty limiting, especially ahorseback. For those fall rides I still favor the warmth and flexibility of my wool union suit underneath, leather chaps over top, and a pair of elkskin gloves with wool liners.

Lost!

It was my third year working for Gene Youderian's V-A ranch, and I knew it was my last. Gene had already made plans for his retirement and was working on a deal to sell his outfitting business.

When he was younger, Gene had been a more ambitious man. He spent years building up his resources and his clientele. Gene had sufficient manpower, mulepower, and horsepower to accommodate dozens of guest trips through the summer, as well as continually occupying two hunting camps for the entirety of the fall hunting season in the Bob Marshall Wilderness.

I had become associated with Gene in the twilight of his outfitting career. The ranch was paid for, the livestock was getting older, and his financial needs, as well as his enthusiasm, were diminishing.

One problem that plagued Gene ever more with the passing years was his bum ankle. He told me a story from his youth of having a wreck with a horse a long way from home. He recounted that it was three days before he was found, laying in a coulee with a broken leg, a punctured lung, and a nasty case of pneumonia.

For a while, he said, they hadn't expected him to live. At that point his twisted leg was not their chief concern. By the time his caregivers were finally confident of his survival, the break had healed in a distorted position.

The misalignment was not a problem for him as a young man; a youthful body can easily compensate for such injuries. But the extra strain placed on the ankle over the years eventually led to deterioration of the joint. By the time I knew the man, walking had become painful and slow.

For this last scheduled hunt in the fall of 1977, Gene had booked several parties. I was assigned with Phil and Brian to the camp at Middle Fork Creek with Verne to do the cooking. My brother Mark went with Gene, Bob, and Cassie into Basin Creek.

We had only four dudes for the trip into Middle Fork. After catering to the usual six or more men in a party, it appeared that this hunt would be a vacation even for the crew. Since half of the mules were needed for Basin Creek, we even had significantly less livestock to be cared for in camp.

With two-thirds as many packs and backs, saddles and stirrups, rifles and riders, we were able to hit the trail an hour sooner in the morning. With twelve mules divvied among three men, our strings were enough shorter that we also made much better time enroute.

It was the first evening in camp that I began to have misgivings about the hunt as Phil began to lay out for us the plans for the next morning. Our party of four was not one group, but rather a pair of buddies and two individuals.

One of the hunters, Phil said, was a cop from Chicago. This man had drawn a Grizzly Bear tag and had paid for a one-man guided hunt. One hunter was a doctor, and his arrogant attitude had already caused a little friction. The other two men had driven together from Wisconsin, and seemed to lack the motivation of the others in camp.

The cop was a pleasant and eager man. He was not of the same financial circumstances as the majority of out-of-state hunters, and had not come the expectation of being catered to. This man was willing to expend whatever energy was required, and to do what ever was asked.

The doctor soon proclaimed himself as a "real" hunter. He had read everything that had ever been printed on the subject of big game, and he was in prime physical shape. The fact that he was traveling alone, however, hinted at his lack of social skills.

The pair from Wisconsin was fairly typical of the class dudes I was used to working with. They had come to Montana for a vacation, and weren't too worried about all the macho details. These two were inclined to linger over their coffee in the morning and over their drinks in the evening.

Because Phil would be taking the cop out alone, I was to be left with the prime responsibility for the other three dudes. This was a new responsibility for me, and I was immediately uncomfortable. I didn't feel competent or qualified to be *leading* the expedition.

Our primary scheme for hunting with Gene had always been the "drive". Each morning he would pick the creek drainage we would work that day, then head out ahorseback with the dudes. Circling around to the head of the drainage before full daylight, Gene would strategically position each hunter in a place where elk were likely to pass when disturbed by an intruder.

My job had always been as "bird dog" - working up the creek on foot, pushing the elk towards the passes where the hunters were stationed. The day's hunt was ended when I reached the hunters on the ridge. Gene had led my horse along with the hunting party, and we all rode back to camp together. I was a neophyte to the Wilderness, and part-time at that. My status was low among professional guides.

Each morning before the dudes were up I would attempt to pick Phil's brain regarding where we should go for the morning hunt. But Phil seemed a little antagonistic toward me. He was concerned mainly with his Grizzly hunter and wasn't willing to give me much help. Brian was new to the area, and I was never sure he would end up where I sent him.

My troubles were further complicated by the fact that while I had been *down* all of the various trails in the daylight, I had never before been *up* them, let alone in the dark. I knew well enough where I wanted to *be*, but I was shaky on how to get there.

When Gene had first recruited me two years before, his main question was "You won't get lost will you?" I was able to assure him, as point of pride, that I had *never* been lost. I have a good sense of direction that had never let me down. In fact, I had outright *contempt* for people who couldn't find their way home.

With as much confidence as I could muster, I led my little group off in search of elk. They had each paid a handsome sum to be there, and I was being paid well also. I was careful not to expose my misgivings to the dudes.

It helped, of course, that the hunters had *no* idea where we were headed. When I stopped to get my bearings, they thought we were just giving the horses a "blow". The hunters never knew when I lost the trail, or when I found it again.

It was only the second day out when the doctor took me aside. He explained to me again that he was a "real" hunter, and complained that the two slobs from Wisconsin were scaring away his elk. He wanted to work separately from them.

I discussed the problem later with Phil, but he offered no sympathy. We didn't have the personnel to conduct a separate hunt for the doc - and anyway, it wasn't Phil's problem.

On the third day out I directed Brian to Crow Creek. I was to take the dudes up to the head of the creek, and he was to act as bird dog. Leading Brian 's horse, I took the dudes and headed out into the dark.

Our timing was right and we hit the Crow Creek ridge just at daylight. We would be working up the back side of the ridge as Brian hiked up the trail from camp to Crow Creek. I would have the hunters placed overlooking the saddles in the ridge-top when Brian made his drive up the creek toward us.

Things were going according to plan until I hit the slide-rock. To reach the ridge-top we had to pick our way through a vast area of stones the size dinner plates. There were dozens of minor game trails through the rock-field, but not the obvious path I was expecting.

I searched the hillside in the meager early morning light and picked the most obvious trail to make our ascent. We made a couple of switch-backs as we worked up the hill, then the trail headed away from our intended destination toward a patch of timber.

This obviously wasn't the right trail, so we rested the horses as I looked for a different path.

The horses clattered and slipped across the slide, struggling to balance the weight of the hunters and their gear, until we struck another trail. My face was red, but I hoped the hunters hadn't noticed.

Our new trail carried us a little further in the proper direction before it, too, petered out.

By now I was sure the hunters were aware that I was lost. But they were more concerned with the precariousness of their positions atop 1400 pound horses which were constantly in danger of losing their footing and rolling down the mountain.

After an hour or more of picking our way across the rock-field we were approaching the top of the ridge. My initial trajectory had been side-tracked numerous times, and we emerged quite a bit lower than I had intended.

I was "resting the horses" and looking for an appropriate route to our destination when we heard an elk bugle!

Lifting the wooden flute that hung on my neck I returned the call. The answer was immediate and close, but the tone was obviously phony - *there were other hunters in the area who were blowing on elk calls.*

That discovery dashed my entire game plan. My mind was racing, trying to figure out what to do next when a bull elk burst out of the timber 40 yards away and disappeared over the ridge in front of us. That phony *sounding* bugle had come from a real elk!

The four of us sat numbly on our horses, rifles still safely in the scabbards, as our quarry had passed in plain sight. I felt my credibility as a guide dropping quickly.

Another whistle from the trees revealed that at least one bull remained nearby. I indicated the group to some nearby trees where we could tie up our horses.

It is incredible how much noise hunters and horses can make in contrast to the sounds of the wilderness. Horseshoes clattered against the rocks, clothing swished, and men and animals grunted as we quickly dismounted and pulled out our rifles.

I split the party up - two on each side of the ridge. The plan was to move as slowly and quietly as possible to circle around the elk that had been whistling his defiance from the forest.

I sent the doc ahead of me and tried to distract the nearby elk with my flute. We both winced when we heard noises from the two Wisconsin buddies on the other side of the ridge.

The elk continued his conversation with me, but he never accepted my challenge. The breeze was in our favor, so I don't think he smelled us, but the bull was suspicious. His calls were moving away faster than doc was closing in.

It was late in the morning before all four of us were reunited at the horses, each with a tale of disappointment. Brian would be emerging soon, a mile or so further west, expecting to find us. I left the hunters to eat their lunches as I took the spare horse and headed out to look for my "bird dog".

This whole trip to the mountains was uncomfortable for me, and I was relieved when it came to an end. But I had yet to put away any meat for my family. Before the season was over I stopped by Frank Thompson's ranch on the Dearborn River to do a little hunting. I didn't have a lot of time to spend, but I could make a quick run up behind Frank's house.

The clouds were very low that day, and spitting snow. Visibility was limited, but the fresh snow absorbed all sound.

I headed out afoot on the north side of a ridge that led straight west upwards toward the continental divide. My position on the ridge gave me full view of the slope to my right, while trees to my left broke up my outline.

Moving slowly, I stopped often to search the landscape, my rifle always ready. There was plenty of sign that deer were around, but they seemed to be brushed up by the weather. I was running out of patience, and getting a little careless, when a fence appeared on my right.

The fence took me by surprise. I wasn't well acquainted with Frank's ranch, but I knew from whence I had come. I hadn't crossed any fence coming up, and it puzzled me to suddenly have one suddenly show up between where I was and where I had been.

As I was pondering where this fence could have come from, I noticed another hunter leaning against a tree a short way off. We visited a bit, and I learned that he was an out-of-state hunter who was a guest of the neighbor, Tag Rittel. Tag had an outfitting business in addition to his cow operation.

I explained to him that I was a local who had just walked up from Frank's place "over there". The fellow said no, Frank's was "over here", and pointed in the opposite direction.

Of course this guy was a dude, so I wasn't too impressed by his contradiction of my mental compass. I just hoped *he* would be able to find his way home.

81

But the combination of the out-of-place fence and the misplaced hunter shook my confidence a little. I left him and continued my trek "up" the ridge, only to discover that the ridge wasn't going _up_ anymore.

It was getting late enough that I needed to head back anyway, so I followed the nearest creek back down the hill. It seemed to be heading in the wrong direction, but water nearly always runs downhill. With such poor visibility, I couldn't see where I wanted to be, but I knew the creek would take me down into _somebody's_ hay meadow.

When Frank's buildings finally appeared out of the curtain of snow, they were backwards also! It took a little figuring to understand what I had done.

Apparently the ridge didn't taper evenly up the mountain. There must have been some sort of pass that allowed me to circle around to the opposite side and continue for a while in the reverse direction with the ridge still on my left.

And so, in the space of two weeks I had been humiliated twice – once in the wilderness where I had been hunting for several seasons, and once on a ranch in the foothills where I was also acquainted. My confidence was shaken, and I became a little more sympathetic to stories of people who had gotten turned around in the woods.

Elk Tracks

For most of the year, the town of Augusta, Montana, is a sleepy little village in the middle of prime ranch country at the foot of the Rocky Mountain Front. In the fall, however, it surges to new life as the Mecca for elk hunters world wide.

For the three months of hunting season the main street is lined with trucks and trailers full of horses, mules, and gear headed to, or returning from, the trails leading over the continental divide into the wilderness. Bearded men crowd the bars to drink and tell hunting stories, and rifles are visible in every direction.

Early bull season in the Bob Marshall and Scapegoat Wilderness opens September 15th. The weather is usually pretty mild yet, and most of the good campsites are occupied. Hunters are scattered throughout the huge expanse of the Rocky Mountains.

Elk season ends about 10 weeks later, somewhere around Thanksgiving. By that time snow has usually pushed both elk and hunters to the lower elevations on the Rocky Mountain Front.

This particular fall my elk tag was still open in late November. I'd heard of some elk on the back side of Lime Reef, so I headed out early one morning to see what I could find.

My headlights found the county road that led across the prairie toward Benchmark, and I bounced over the gravel in the dark. It took about 45 minutes to reach the place where Willow Creek breaks out at the foot of the Rockies. There was a faint glow in the eastern sky as I grabbed my rifle and a sack of jerky and started out afoot, headed straight north on the back side of the reef.

The temperature was near zero as the day dawned. I wanted to be a few miles from the road by shooting light, and anyway, I had to keep moving just to keep from freezing. By the time the sun was high enough to radiate a little warmth, I had gained a lot of elevation.

It was a beautiful clear day. The thin snow cover was crisp, dry, and bright; there wasn't another human being for miles. The sparse trees were gnarled and twisted from their continuous battle with the wind.

For several hours I hunted, checking out each patch of brush and each grove of quaking aspen, before I finally cut sign. It was probably a young bull, I figured from the tracks, since the trail showed the elk to be alone.

I didn't know for sure how fast I should proceed. The tracks had been made sometime that morning, I couldn't tell for sure when. I could be minutes - or hours - behind the animal that made them. If the bull had come through in the dark, I might never catch up to him. And if I hurried, I might overtake and spook him.

While I was in the midst of pondering the situation, a sage hen exploded out of the trees about 30 yards to my right, and flew across in front of me. I was a little puzzled that the bird had flushed at that great a distance from me, but I was eager to see where the elk track led.

Resuming my pursuit, I followed the prints along the edge of the quakers. Suddenly I realized that the tracks circled around to my right. My heart began to pound. There was no question, now, about when those tracks had been made. The elk that was making them had just spooked that bird!

It is amazing that an animal as large as an elk can move so silently. A huge bull can tilt his head back to lay his antlers over his shoulders, and noiselessly navigate through brush that a man cannot penetrate. Many hunters have been close enough to an elk in the brush that they could smell his musky odor - and still never see him.

One on one with an elk is exciting and dramatic, but discouraging. No matter how quiet and alert a man is, his senses are but a fraction as keen as those of his prey. The elk is in his element and pretty much controls the hunt. It is common for an elk to circle back as this one had done, to get a look at his pursuer.

I spent an hour or more stalking the bull without ever catching sight nor sound of him. It was obvious that he knew my every move and had no intention of exposing himself to me. I would have to use my one organ which was - in theory - superior to his: my brain.

Quitting the track, I headed straight west, up and over the ridge that parallels Lime Reef. Out of range of the elk's eyes and ears I was free to move undetected. The bull had been moving north toward Home Gulch; my idea was to circle around and cut him off.

I moved north at a pretty good clip. Every so often I would top the ridge and spend some time glassing the area below trying to catch a glimpse of my quarry, but still nothing. When I felt sure that I was ahead of the elk, I climbed back over the ridge and began to hunt back in the direction from which I had come that morning.

It had been hours since I had seen my elk, and I was tired. With no tracks to follow, finding that elk again was like looking for a gopher in a hay field. I was a long way from home and the sun was getting lower in the sky. Finally I gave up on the hunting, threw my gun over my shoulder, and began hiking in earnest toward my vehicle.

Suddenly I heard a crashing in the trees ahead of me. I ran in the direction of the sound. Thirty yards away I found in the snow the print of the elk's body where he had been laying, watching his back-trail. The tracks leading from the bed were about 10 feet apart and headed straight down the mountainside. He was as surprised to hear me as I was to hear him!

I could hear the startled elk busting through a pole thicket, now a hundred yards away. He had given up stealth, and was headed down Home gulch as fast as his long legs could carry him.

It was already dark down in the valley shadows. To try to follow that elk now would be futile. There was no reasonable choice but to allow that bull to live for another year. I would have to be satisfied with telling the story about another one that had gotten away.

Dry Cleaning

I had been working all day on the rear end of a truck. Artie's ranch had no real shop facilities, so I located in the best shade I could find - on the ground under the truck bed. The smelly old gear oil permeated my clothing as I worked over, under, around, and through the filthy old differential .

My wife had gone to a church gathering for a few days, so my two young daughters had spent the day at work with me. They weren't too happy to be riding home in the same pickup with me. First priority on my arrival home was to take a shower and change into clean clothes.

Emerging from the shower with a clean nose, I was met by the offensive odor and the crusty appearance of the shirt that I'd been wearing. Barb had made it for me and it was still too nice to be ruined by grease. Gear oil is awful stuff, and I contemplated how I might wash it out of my clothes. I couldn't see how detergent alone would take it out of my garments.

Gasoline was the stuff, I decided, and I poured some into a tub, over the filthy clothes. But still considering, I didn't figure that it would do to let the gasoline evaporate - that would leave the grease right where it was. The only solution was to wash the gas and oil out together.

So I stirred the clothes around in the gas for awhile, then wrung them out and threw them in the automatic washer with a big helping of detergent. That done, I went out to pull a few weeds in the garden.

I hadn't been outside long when I was startled by a terrific WHUMP! The girls came screaming out of the house and I ran in to see what had happened. I quickly put out the flaming broom that sat across the hall from the washing machine, then looked around to assess the damage.

The lid was up on the machine. There was a little bow in it, but no real damage. The broom was scorched but functional. Everything else in the area seemed unharmed. When I closed the lid, the spin cycle resumed.

It didn't take me long to figure out what happened: hot water pouring into the washer had vaporized the gasoline. The next time a relay had clicked, the spark set off the fumes.

I'm sure my wife would have used a different method - mine was a bit unconventional. But nothing was destroyed, it didn't cost much, and my clothes came out spotlessly clean!

Bears!

A true cowboy always prefers to be ahorseback. But sometimes he has to leave his horse behind and do a job *afoot*. Such was the case the day I was fixing fence at the "mountain land".

Artie and his father summered their cattle in a pasture on the East Slope of the Continental Divide. The field borders on Highway 200 which runs from Great Falls to Lincoln, crossing the Divide at Rogers Pass.

The terrain of this pasture gets fairly steep, with large areas of grass running into the forest. The upper parts of the fence peter out in the rocks and trees towards the top of the divide.

On one pleasant day in early June, I was assigned the task of checking the fence, just prior to our trailing the cattle up into the pasture for the summer. As most of the job would be done from the window of a four-wheel-drive pickup, it seemed a good project in which to include my two daughters. Amy and Wendy must have been 5 and 4 years old respectively, and they accompanied me on the trip. We had lunch and a water bottle, and looked forward to a pleasant day in the mountains.

It was about 30 miles to the pasture from the ranch. Once we got to the field, we simply picked our way along the fence in the pickup looking for breaks in the wire.

There were places where posts had rotted off, and there were places where the snow had drifted over and broken the fence. Trees and branches had fallen across the wires, and wildlife had run through it. At each break in the fence I would shut off the pickup and repair the damage while the girls explored the area nearby.

Near the top of the fence I had to quit the pickup and head out afoot. I carried a coil of wire, a few staples, hammer, fence pliers, and fence stretcher. The girls tagged along.

It was getting steep and rocky, and near the end of the fence. The cows had no reason to come this high, so the fence just stopped a little further on. I told the girls they could stay where they were, picking wild strawberries, and I'd be back down in a few minutes. Continuing along, I spliced a wire here, and put in a staple there.

Then I saw the bear.

It was a yearling, I judged - just pushed out of the winter's den by a new arrival to the family. His coat was rather scruffy and he looked lean and hungry.

Bears are assumed to be near-sighted, and this one hadn't yet seen me. The wind was in my favor and neither had he caught my scent. I was enjoying watching him in his search for food: looking under rocks and tearing apart rotting logs. This was one of the benefits of ranch life: being able to observe the local wildlife close up.

There was no reason for me to have any fear of the animal. He was a Black Bear cub who meant no one harm. Any minute now he would notice me, and be gone in a hurry.

Then I heard the girls scream!

The cub was no danger to anyone. But his mother would be a different matter. An angry cow can inflict enough damage with her head on anything disturbing her young; a mama *bear* has long teeth and claws!

I looked around for a weapon of some kind. The fence pliers in my hand had a hard point, and they seemed to be the best thing I could find. I headed back down the mountain as quickly as I could, intent on protecting my young.

When I entered the clearing where I had left the girls, I quickly searched the area for Mama bear. I saw nothing. Thankful that the girls appeared unharmed, I hurried over to them.

"What's wrong?" I asked as I gathered them to me. To which the two little girls replied:

"We got l-o-n-e-l-y."

Muddin'

Yeager's upper place west of Choteau was good cow country. It had plenty of water near the surface to irrigate the hayfields and the brush patches. We put up plenty of feed during the summer, and the brush made the best kind of protection from the winter winds. In the "swamp" field, the water was even more plentiful and closer to the surface. It made good summer grazing, but the mud made it hard for a horse to get around.

One day we had some cow business out in the swamp. I saddled Prince and King, and Wendy and I headed out. I had traded Gene Youderian out of an old kid's saddle when I had been shoeing and guiding for him - it was small and light, just right for such a little girl.

We hadn't gotten far past the gate when we got in a bit of a tight spot. We didn't yet know the country well, and we found ourselves in a particularly boggy meadow. There was nothing to do but keep slogging along until we could reach firmer ground. At the age of 5, Wendy was already an accomplished cowgirl and could follow wherever I went. The horses knew the terrain better than we, and just lunged on through the mud.

When I heard a yelp from behind, I looked back. There lay Wendy on her back in the mud, with the saddle still clamped between her legs. The cinch had broke!

This little saddle had never been much. It was made of thin Mexican leather over a cloth covered wooden tree. It was cheap, but it had stirrups and it had kept Wendy's butt clean. It had worked fine for Wendy while we were riding the prairie country south of Augusta.

I climbed off my horse, trying to stand on the grassy tufts out of the muck. I sat Wendy on my horse while I put her riggin' back together.

With a little work with my pocket knife and pieces of leather cut off *my* saddle strings, I got her saddle tied down again. Wendy scrambled across the horse's backs to her former perch atop old King. We were ready to go.

I picked my way back around to Prince, stuck my muddy foot in the stirrup, and swung up on his back. But King stood a little too close, and I caught him with my off foot right upside of the head. King sucked back in pain and fear, the cinch broke in a different place, and Wendy found herself lying in the mud again.

The next trip to town we found a good used kid's saddle that would stand up to the kind of riding that a <u>real</u> cowgirl would be doing.

Coyote Fur

One evening in the early 70's in the Bears Paw Mountains we stopped by Les Morgan's place one evening to visit. He and his wife had a trailer house set up in the middle of prime coyote country and spent the winter trapping. Pelts of any kind were bringing pretty good money at the time, and trapping was a profitable enterprise.

There was a woodstove on the porch, and Les was busy with a hide that was inside out on the elongated triangular stretching frame. I stepped up to inspect his work and found him carefully stitching up a seven-inch gash right down middle of the coyote's forehead. He was using two needles and nylon thread to make a neat baseball stitch pulling the hide together. Finishing up the job, Les picked up his coffee cup, leaned back, and told us the story.

He had been out checking traps that day and topped a rise to startle a coyote along the creek. As the coyote sped away, Les had drawn a bead on the back of its head with his .222 and fired. The coyote had dropped in his tracks.

There was no sign of life when Les reached the downed animal, so he grabbed it by the hind legs and slung it over his shoulder.

As he was walking back to the pickup, Les felt movement behind him, and heard the snapping jaws of an angry coyote right at the most tender part of his backside. Apparently the bullet had just *creased* the varmint's skull and knocked him cold.

With a mighty heave, Les flung the coyote down on the ground full length in front of him and stood on its ribcage until he was quite sure the animal was dead.

Five years later I had occasion to set out some traps. We had lost a cow, and I had drug it with a tractor out to the edge of the swamp. I set out several traps around the carcass in hopes of catching some Christmas money.

This swamp was located about 15 miles west of Choteau, a part of what is now the Pine Butte Game Preserve owned by Nature's Conservancy. It was a pretty wild area. Coyotes were plentiful and grizzly bears weren't uncommon even then.

The next day after the cows were fed I headed over in the pickup to check my traps. Sure enough, I had one! Grabbing a club, I headed over to dispatch the critter that was caught by one leg.

But as I approached, the coyote found new strength. Lunging to the end of the chain, the animal pulled free and bounded off into the brush.

Disappointed, I reset the trap. It was below zero and the wind was blowing in fresh snow. I used my feet to form a ridge of snow a few inches upwind of the trap, knowing that it would soon drift over and be hidden by fresh dry snow.

My camouflage must have worked as planned because the next day when I returned there was another coyote in the trap. I had lost one critter, but I had learned. Pulling my trusty .308 from behind the seat, I laid the gun over the hood of the pickup and placed a bullet right at the base of the coyote's skull.

Back at the barn I quickly undressed the animal. With a slit from one hind foot clear across to the other, I was able to peel the hide off inside out just as a boy pulls off his shirt. The stretching frame made of two 1x2's joined at the nose was ready for me to lay on the fresh pelt. I pulled the legs down snug and tacked them, then spread the slats to take the slack out of the sides.

Before the hide was too dry I sat down to patch the bullet hole. The entrance was but a third of an inch in diameter and took only 3 stitches. The exit was a different story.

The cartridge I had used was meant for big game. The heavy bullet was designed to mushroom on impact and do enough damage to drop a thousand-pound elk in his tracks. The hole it had made coming out of the coyote was about the size and shape of my hand.

Winter nights are long in Montana, and I had nowhere to go. I set about the repair job calmly and patiently. With fine, even stitches, I slowly worked down each finger of the torn skin, pulling the hide back into its general original shape. There were a few pieces of the puzzle that didn't fit; so I cut them off and threw them away, counting on the natural stretch of the skin to make up the slight differences in shape. I was pretty happy with the result and left it on the porch to finish drying.

It was a few weeks later that I saw the opportunity to go to town. The weather was good, the work was caught up, and I'd gotten my monthly paycheck. I stopped by the house to tell my wife to start getting ready while I fed the calves.

Into the back of the pickup we threw the tire chains, a scoop shovel, and a few blankets in a plastic bag. I pulled the coyote and the beaver pelts off their stretchers, cleaned them up, and threw them in too.

The first stop in Great Falls was Pacific Hide and Fur Depot. The amount of money we received there would determine the extent of our activities on this trip. The Beaver was big and prime, and brought $35. I was a little anxious over the coyote pelt after having blown such a big hole in the neck. "You must have shot this one; Seventy-five dollars," announced the buyer after looking the hide over.

I was very pleasantly surprised. "How much would it have been worth if I <u>hadn't</u> shot him?" I asked. "No difference," he said. "You must have done a good job sewing him up. The only way I knew you shot him was the patch of ice on his neck where you washed the blood off."

For a while in the seventies, trapping was big winter business. There were people who spent the winter on snowmobiles running down coyotes on the frozen prairies. The revenue from the hides paid for the machines and left the hunters with a good living.

Wages at the time were around $450/month. That fur money sure looked good by comparison. But I had a hard time reconciling my conscience over killing animals solely for hides that would be used purely for luxury rather than necessity. The only other pelt I ever sold was that of a fox that had been struck by a vehicle while crossing the road.

Blowing Snow

Winter blew in with a fury in October of 1978. We had only recently weaned the cattle, and there were 600 sad calves bawling in my corrals.

That first storm lasted only one day. It was hard to measure the actual snowfall, as it had come in horizontally - the ground was bare in some places, and the snow was three feet deep in others.

Out in the hayfields the cows had plenty of dry grass to eat. This soon after having their calves taken away the cows were still more concerned with their loss than they were with eating. The brush along the creeks offered plenty of protection from the wind.

The snowstorm was a rather rude way for fall to end, but the sun soon came out. Mud replaced the snow, and the wind dried the ground. We trailed the cows to the home ranch, and turned the calves out to pasture.

Storms increased in frequency and intensity as November blew through. A pattern began to emerge of 3-day storms followed by a week of good weather, and the snow started to pile up in places.

The ranch buildings that my growing family inhabited were located just off the county road, 15 miles west of Choteau. Because it was a school bus route, this gravel road was one of the first to be plowed after a snow.

Roads in Montana are nearly all built up with material taken from the "borrow" pits on both sides of the right-of-way. Continuous winds blowing off the Rocky Mountain Front sweep the snow off the elevated surface and into the borrow pit along most of the routes. But where the roads cut through a hill or drop down into a coulee the snow can accumulate.

As the winter progressed, the ditches began to fill with snow. Each pass of a snowplow threw more snow up along the side of the road. Any irregularity in the surface along the roadside will catch some snow, and drifts began to build in sheltered places.

Down around the ranch buildings the snow was piling up. After each storm I used the big loader tractor to scoop the snow out of the thoroughfares so I could get through to haul hay to the cattle.

With each successive plowing, the drifts got deeper on both sides of the road. Even after the snow stopped, the wind continued to rearrange the landscape, filling in the gaps that had just been plowed through the drifts.

On my occasional trips to town, I wondered at the plowing process that had become a daily chore for the road crew. I watched as the one-way plows threw the snow off the road and into the wind, only to see it blown right back on the road.

The wind in North Central Montana blows predominantly out of the west. A southbound plow throws the snow upwind in a temporary gesture. Any snow that stays on the west side of the road serves only to catch more snow and make a deeper drift across the road.

It has always seemed counterproductive to me to plow into the wind. I figured the truck just as well deadhead south, and only drop the plow on the return trip north. Our good friend Gilbert Sangray had worked for the county for years, so I asked him about the practice.

The reason the road crews plowed snow into the wind was simple, Gilbert said over a cup of coffee: overtime! Plowing snow from the nice warm cab of a modern truck was a good way to earn Christmas money.

When Gilbert had worked for the county it was on salary. That arrangement was a powerful incentive toward efficiency. Any plowing that needed to be done of an evening or weekend was simply a part of the job, and kept a man away from his family with no additional compensation.

Fence pliers had been a standard item in Gilbert's truck, he said. Many's the time he had let down the fence to plow up drift berms out in a field to catch the snow *before* it got to the road.

As this winter progressed, the drifts got deeper. With each storm it took longer to get the roads opened up again. During a lull in the weather, my parents drove in to visit during Christmas.

The night they arrived it was clear and cold - 22° below zero. As soon as we had all their gear carried in from the van, I went out to put it away in a shed.

The arctic cold had already cooled the engine off and made it sluggish; I ran the battery down trying to get it started. Trudging through the snow in the dark, I returned with a battery charger and plugged it in for the night.

In the morning I had cattle to feed – a job that took up half the day. It was mid-afternoon before I had time to go check out the van. The battery was charged and ready for another attempt, and I turned the key.

With a fresh charge and a booster, the rig cranked pretty well. But it didn't offer to start. The oil was stiff, and batteries lose efficiency quickly in the cold. With no help at all from the engine, we soon ran out of juice and had to put the charger back on.

Next day was a repeat of the one before, and we returned to the van in the fading light of the afternoon. This time we checked the plugs to make sure we had spark. The ignition was fine, and there was gas to the carburetor. But again we drained the battery before the engine ever fired.

On the third afternoon we checked the compression and the timing. We found nothing amiss, yet the engine refused to respond. With a standard transmission we'd have pulled it down the road and made it go, but the automatic killed that idea.

For six days my folks visited. And for six days we tried to start their outfit.

We'd tried pumping the carburetor, we'd tried holding the throttle to the floor. We even tried starting fluid. For nearly a week we'd not gotten so much as a pop from the stubborn engine. It was just too cold.

Nearly every rig in Montana is outfitted with an engine heater, but this van had none. There was no heated garage on the place to warm the rig up. I had run out of ideas.

The battery was charged again, but I had no real hope as I turned the key. We had already tried everything I could think of. The weather was still cold, and there was no break in sight.

But as the starter turned the engine over one more time, I heard it pick up a beat! Then another, and another. It coughed, and sputtered, and complained; but it kept running!

With the setting of the sun the wind began to pick up. I left the rig running as we packed the folk's gear and ate supper. By the time we had the outfit loaded and ready to go the snow was drifting across the road.

As deep as the snow was piled along the road, I knew that we'd be drifted in by morning. It was time for the folks to get while the gettin' was good.

I got the four-wheel drive pickup out of the shed and gave last minute instructions to Dad. With only two-wheel drive and no chains, he'd have to keep up his speed to get through the snow that was blowing across the road. I would break trail for him if he could keep the rig straight behind me.

It was really a beautiful night for a drive. The temperature had warmed to a balmy 20° above and the stars shown crisply from the night sky. Even the ground blizzard was a thing of beauty - the whole clean white world moving sideways as far as we could see.

The road was hard to pick out under the headlight's glare on the blowing snow. Finger drifts were growing across our path.

Dad pulled in behind me and kept in sight of my taillights as I headed for town. His rig slowed and slewed when he struck the drifts through which I had just opened a trail, but he motored on.

To my folks it appeared that I was traveling across a bare sweep of prairie with nothing to guide me. But I knew that the road lay precisely between the fences. And were I to misjudge my position, I would merely slide down into the soft dry snow that filled the ditches.

I was still young and invincible - I saw the trip as an adventure. It never occurred to me that my folks might be afraid of being swallowed up by the dark and the cold, never to be seen alive again.

Town was a little farther away than I had remembered it to be, and even _I_ was glad to see its lights. But we'd made the trip without mishap.

The state highway was still blowing clear, and the reflec-tors along the roadside made it much easier to follow. I stayed in the lead until we topped the ridge a few miles south of Choteau.

Pulling off at the first turnout, I walked back to confer with my parents.

Snowplows would not run again until morning, and the drifts would continue to grow until then. To beat the drifting snow, the folks would have to keep moving until they got out of the Chinook Country, another 50 miles south.

Gilbert and Rose Sangray lived in Augusta, 25 miles down the highway. I knew that they would put on a pot of coffee for the travelers, and give them good advice on driving conditions.

Dad was worried about my heading back out to the ranch. Our tracks through the drifts had blown in soon after we passed, and there would be no other traffic to offer me aid if I were to get stuck.

But my tire chains and scoop shovel were in the back of the pickup, and I had on enough clothes to weather the elements. I would reach the ranch about the same time they reached Augusta; we could check up on each other by phone.

There wasn't so much snow further on south and the folks made Augusta with no problems. Gilbert and Rose offered re-freshment for both body and soul, then sent them on down the highway and away from the wind.

When my folks arrived back home they had quite a story to tell. They had lived through a siege of real Montana weather, and had enough adventure to keep them content for a few more months.

Ropin'

During calving at Yeager's Y Slash H ranch, I drew the job of doctoring calves. I couldn't quite understand how I was selected, but I wasn't complaining - I never complained about any work that got me ahorseback.

I'd been riding Prince all winter. He was a big sorrel Thoroughbred/Quarter Horse cross that Harry had taken in trade on one of his purebreds. Yeagers had a registered Quarter Horse stud, and cutting horses.

When I first started riding Prince he made me nervous. The horse was big and powerful, and cut into his turns a little harder than I trusted him. But I was assured that he had never gone down, so I learned to relax and lean into the corners with him.

Prince had a stance that was reminiscent of a football lineman; his hind legs spraddled. As I got better acquainted with him I learned that he was an excellent cow horse, and I suspected that it was this base-wide stance that gave him such stability. He could cut cattle in the worst of footing without ever losing his balance. Prince was big, strong, intelligent, and athletic. I liked him.

We'd moved all the cows from the upper place to the home place for calving, and I'd taken Prince along to use in the spring work. He'd been my horse all winter, and I continued to use him doctoring calves.

I timed my "house calls" for just after feeding. For about two hours after the hay had been spread out in a long line through the field the cows would all be gathered along the row with their heads down. I could ride slowly up the line, looking over each cow and each calf for signs of trouble.

Prince understood the game and walked quietly through the herd. When I'd find a calf to treat, we'd ease him out of the bunch toward the open prairie. The calf would generally be 20 feet away from the feed before he realized that he was alone with a horse on his trail. When the calf made his break, I had a loop ready. Prince needed no guidance put me right up for a throw, and we generally had the calf caught within a few jumps.

My scours boluses and balling gun were in the saddle bags along with a paint-stick. I could give the calf a couple of pills, mark him, and turn him loose without disturbing the rest of the cattle nearby. And so we worked up the line until we had seen all the cattle and doctored anything that was sick.

As with any antibiotic, it is necessary to give a full course of treatment of scours medication. If the treatment ends before the bugs are all dead, the remaining bacteria develop an immunity. And sometimes one medication doesn't work on a particular animal and another type must be given.

So I used different colors of paint in different places on the calf to document my medical history. A red stripe for Terramycin down the face on Monday; across the nose on Tuesday, across the forehead on Wednesday. On Thursday I could use blue paint-stick and start all over again. For Penicillin I might put a circle around an eye, or an X on the nose. And so I could read the course of each calf's treatment.

One day Harry said to me in his rapid-fire way, "You can't keep camping on just one horse. You never know when we'll need more horses, and we have to keep them all hard. I want you to ride Trigger every other day." So the next day I left Prince in the corral and saddled Trigger - a registered Quarter Horse - to make my daily round.

One of the things I learned about genetics in college is the effect of "hybrid vigor". Anytime you cross one purebred animal with one of another line of breeding you get an automatic 10% increase in performance. Practically speaking, the only reason to have pure breeds is to have separate genetic lines from which to cross.

Since my intent was always to have a horse to *ride* rather than a horse to *breed*, there was never any reason for me to have a purebred. And besides, I'd never had much use for paying the premium for a registered horse. As they say, "You can't ride the papers".

But Yeagers had some pretty good horses, bred for cutting. This was the first papered Quarter Horse I had ever ridden. And I wasn't given a choice.

Prince and I had our system down pat. We could get our job done with a minimum of chousing and fuss. But when I nosed out the first calf to catch and doctor with Trigger, it quickly became obvious that I would have to teach this new horse how I worked.

We began as I always had, right after the cattle had been fed. Trigger and I started up the line looking for signs of sickness. So far, so good.

When we came to the first calf that needed attention, I turned him away from the bunch. He had taken a few steps before he understood that a horse and rider were in pursuit. When the calf broke and ran, I nudged my horse and prepared to lay on a loop.

But the calf was pulling away. I kicked the horse harder in an attempt to get close enough for a throw, but the calf had already circled back and gotten lost in the herd.

As Harry had said, we needed to keep all the horses hard. Trigger was out of shape physically, and he hadn't had enough riding to keep his handling in shape either. It would take awhile to tune him up.

As we again tried to work our way up the line of cattle, Trigger was fidgety. The adrenaline rush from the little run had gotten him hyped up. The horse's agitation was sensed by the herd. The cows got nervous and began to pick up their calves and take them away from the feed and toward the safety of the brush.

The next day I was back on Prince. If anything, the rest had done him good. He was quick and eager, and we made up for yesterday's lost time. Prince could <u>feel</u> which calf I had picked out, and in just a few strides I was in position to rope. I was able to take my mind off of guiding the horse and concentrate solely on the aim of my loop.

Prince and I had a lot of fun with the job, and we did it together in a very efficient manner.

But the next day it was Trigger's turn again. He didn't seem to have learned anything from our last go. When I started a calf out of the herd I would have to use my rope to "over and under" the horse to get within range of the calf. It took a lot more running and a lot more commotion for each calf we had to doctor. I was aggravated, the horse was aggravated, and worst of all, the cows were aggravated. The extra chousing was hard on the calves, and it caused the cows to quit the feed before I'd had a chance to see all the calves.

Swapping horses made the job harder for me. On Trigger, I had to keep a firm hold on the reins and always be aiming the horse. My roping suffered from my divided attention. If I ever kicked Prince, like I did Trigger, as we moved out after a calf, he would really jump out, sometimes throwing me over the back of the saddle.

Some horses understand the game, others don't. Trigger never did get the picture. More times than one I would leave the herd behind a black calf, circle clear back around before I could catch him, blow through the feeding cattle, and emerge following, a red calf.

No horse is tops at every job, but I never did find out what really suited Trigger. I've since ridden more papered Quarter Horses and my opinion has never changed. Like one old horseman told a tenderfoot who was aghast at riding a horse whose lineage had never been documented, "You can just take those papers and wipe your ass with them, then get on this horse!"

Sonic Boom

"Foot Rot" is a common affliction of light-skinned cattle in the summer. An otherwise minor injury to a foot can allow invasion of bacteria, followed by infection and swelling, finally leaving the animal lame.

Treatment for the condition is a course of antibiotic therapy given by injection, by oral medication, or both. The medication is readily available, reasonably priced, easily administered, and highly effective. The only limiting factor is the lack of cooperation from the patient.

When the invalids are younger cattle out on summer range, treatment can be pure fun for a pair of cowboys. One man ropes the head, the other catches the heels, and the critter is stretched out and helpless on the ground. It was from such routine ranch jobs that the sport of team roping was born.

The most efficient mode of roping is for the pursuing horse to "rate" a running animal at an appropriate distance while his rider lays a flat loop over its head or horns. The "header" then pulls the animal in a circle to the left as the "heeler" lays his upright loop in ahead of the hind legs. The movement of the animal pulls the legs into the "trap", and the animal is caught. The horses are turned to face each other, and back up against the ropes with the animal between them.

Older cattle can be more of a problem. A sore-footed cow is likely to hole up in the brush and "hook" at anyone who approaches. It is much harder to snare a head that is looking at you than one which is running away. Overhanging limbs can obscure the view and snag the loop.

And if you do beat the odds and snare the head, setting the heel rope can be even more of a problem. Range cows are about the same size as a horse, and they are not broke to lead. Laying a good heel trap, and forcing the cow to step into it, can test the patience of a saint.

On one occasion I had spotted a Charolais bull whose foot was raw and swollen. He was in a field near headquarters, and at the time I had neither the manpower nor the horsepower to attempt roping the huge beast in the field. I elected to ride out and bring him to the corrals for treatment.
In the cool of the morning, the bull moved well. I didn't crowd him, and let him rest as often as he chose. The trip to the corrals was uneventful. When the bull was secure in the pen, I rode to the house for the proper equipment.

Returning to the corrals, I tied up my horse and prodded the bull up the chute toward the heavy iron squeeze at the end. The "chute" was a narrow alleyway made of railroad ties set in the dirt with poles nailed on the inside. I quickly discovered that it was designed just wide enough for cows to move through single file; the bull soon became wedged.

This was a big bull - well over a ton. As he struggled between the poles it became apparent that the ties were not set too deeply in the ground. My dog worked over the bull's heels, urging him further up the chute, but there just wasn't enough room for him to pass.

My plan had been to immobilize the bull in the squeeze-chute at the end of the alley, then give him a big injection of long acting penicillin in one end, and a couple of boluses of long acting terramycin in the other. But he became wedged in the chute a long way from the head-gate. Seeing that he was stuck there, I drew my loaded syringe and gave him 25cc in each hip.

112

The bull bawled with the indignity of his treatment and worked his way up a few more inches as the chute swayed and groaned.

Unable to force him up into the head-catch, I snagged his nostrils with the nose-tongs and tied his massive head up to a post. As I read the instructions on the box of antibiotic boluses I made a quick calculation: 1 pill for each 250 pounds....well over 2000 pounds.....almost 10 of these thumb-sized pills. I looked at the single-shot balling gun, and I looked at the bull. Then I headed for the shop.

Under the work bench I found a length of plastic pipe. In the corner was a piece of hose. A picture formed in my mind.

Back at the corral I forced the pipe down the bull's throat. After inserting 4 boluses in the pipe, I tamped with the rubber hose. Another 4 boluses and tamp again. The last two boluses were in when the bull coughed - I had to pick the slobbery pills up off the ground and tamp them *again.*

My mission completed, I was finished with the bull. I pulled out the poles I had placed behind him and fanned my hat in his face. But the bull had on a good mad. He was more interested in getting *at* me than *away* from me.

Picking up a small fence post, I stuck it between the poles and poked the angry bull in the face.

As I said, this was a big bull. His head weighed more than my entire body. You wouldn't believe that something that massive could move quickly. But he gave a snort, and with the speed of light he bunted the post that I was shoving at him.

The force of his explosion propelled the post back toward me with a speed that broke the sound barrier! I saw a black curtain punctuated by yellow stars as the post caught the side of my face and knocked me to the ground.

I was nauseated and dizzy as I lay in the dust trying to gather my senses. I was afraid of what I might feel if I touched my fingers to my cheek.

My horse was standing tied nearby, and I struggled to my feet beside him. The effort of pulling myself into the saddle caused my head to throb even more. But the horse was gentle and the house was close.

Each of the horse's footsteps reverberated in my skull as we eased across the yard. Dropping the reins at the porch I slowly made my way inside.

For the rest of the day I lay in a chair with an icepack on my face, contemplating the power that could move that huge head with such lightning speed.

Tight Quarters

I had a cow that had somehow gotten down country aways – far enough that I elected to take the pickup rather than just ride out and trail her home.

Not everyone had a stock trailer in the 1970s, and slide-in stockracks were common. Sam was my main horse at the time, and he had ridden many a mile in the back of my pickup. Usually I looked for a bank to back up to, or low spot to drop my rear wheels into to make it easier for him to jump in. But with a little encouragement, he could jump clear up into the back of that ¾ ton pickup on flat ground.

So I tipped the stock-rack in, loaded Sam, and headed for the part of the range where my stray cow was reported to be. It didn't take long to find her, and to run her into a little corral in a corner of the field.

I got to studying the situation as I prepared to load the cow. It was about 10 miles around on a country 'two-track" to get home. If I loaded the cow first I would have to make a return trip for the horse. That would be extra trip, extra time, extra fuel .... And there *was* enough room for them both....

A pickup box is 8 feet long and 6 feet wide - plenty of room for two animals to stand side-by-side. In fact, I had hauled two horses a few times. The extra weight made it a little hard to steer, but I wasn't going down the interstate. And the wheel-wells projecting into the floor make it hard for two horses to keep their balance well – but we weren't going far. A plan was forming...

Out on the prairie I found a place where it was easy enough to load Sam. With the horse loaded, I backed up to the loading chute at the corral. With Sam tied in the corner of the stock-rack, I opened the endgate and ran the cow up beside him.

The ride home was a little erratic – cows and horses aren't used to being in such close proximity. The cow would swing her head around at the horse, and the horse would kick at the cow. The only thing that holds a slide-in rack down is the weight of the animals on the floor. If that cow tried to jump out she could tip the whole works over the side.

We made it, however, and saved an hour by doing it all in one trip. No one was injured and nothing was broken. But it was sure hard to load Sam the next time we had somewhere to go with that pickup and stockrack.

On the Fight!

When Marvin bought the Peters place just out of Bynum, there were no cows in the deal, so he attended every livestock auction in the area for several months until we had enough cattle to stock the place. He'd hired me to run things for him. As each truckload came in I ran the cows through the chute to put on his TN Quarter Circle brand.

Buying cattle at a sale ring can be a bit risky. Of course there are a lot of good cattle that go through, but very few of them are the <u>best</u> of someone else's herd. They come from all sizes of herds, and all kinds of places, under all kinds of management, with all kinds of genetics. We had every color, and shape, and size, and disposition.

Working among this put-together bunch was a challenge. Some were flighty cattle that had been herded with pickups and motorcycles. Others had been handled only by a man afoot. Every little group reacted differently when I rode through ahorseback.

Moving these cattle was a treat! None of the cows knew what to expect or where we were headed when we trailed them out a gate. There was no herd bond to keep them together, and no old cows to lead the group. Some ran from a horse, and some only stood and stared. They looked for any opportunity to scatter.

We had a few wrecks that summer, but no one got hurt. I kept a close eye on the cows and culled them hard at every opportunity. By the next spring the herd was beginning to shape up.

I had 275 cows at calving time - quite a few more than what the facilities were designed for. Things were a little more western than how Peters had done when he owned the place - but that's the way I liked it.

My calving field was right behind the house. It was too small to put all those cows in at once, so I cut in whatever was starting to look heavy. The "outside" cows were in a field down the lane and across the road, only half a mile from the buildings.

The best time to have a good close look at your cattle is when they're strung out eating hay. A guy can ease down through them and eyeball each one. If you move through them quietly, you can take one out of the bunch without disturbing them, then come right back to where you left off.

I cut the heavies out every few days. I could usually get my wife to bring the truckload of hay down while I rode my horse. I could feed the hay in a long line, then climb on my horse to cut out those which were close to calving.

The cows still didn't know my routine, but it was fairly easy to cut one out of the bunch and push her through the gate and across the road to where I had spread a little hay to hold the cut.

One particular cow challenged my plan. She didn't have much respect for me or my horse. But I was riding Dude, as good a cow horse as a guy could want.

Every time the cow tried to turn back to the herd, Dude and I were in front of her. She ducked, and spun, and tried to run away, and we were always right with her. Dude and I were both grinning. We loved it when we got some real action! But the cow got mad.

When she quit yielding to our presence and turning away from us, Dude threw a shoulder into her to make her turn. Finally she got serious and just charged through us to get back to the group.

Most of the year that lariat just hangs on the saddle for decoration. A rope can get a guy into more trouble than it can get him out of. It doesn't often pay to rope a cow when you're alone, but this cow was going where I wanted her to go!

When Dude saw that rope uncoil, he knew just what to do. As soon as I gave him his head, he lined up my right knee with her left hip - and kept it there until I dropped a loop over her head.

Now this was a big cow, and Dude was just an average size horse. With one end of the rope down on her shoulders and the other end dallied up high over his withers, the old girl had all the mechanical advantage. We would only be able to pull her a few feet with brute force, and it would result only in the cow being choked down.

But we could keep her from going the wrong way. Standing between her and the herd, we gave her some slack, and waited. When she decided to move in the right direction, we followed. When she chose the wrong direction, we jerked her up short. It took awhile, but we got the job done - the cow was finally with the cut across the road.

The fun wasn't over yet. We still had to get the rope off her neck.

Alone, a guy has a couple of choices: he can ride up beside her and pull the loop off over her head; or he can choke her down, get off his horse, pull off the rope, and get back on the horse before she gets up. But my wife and kids were there in the truck watching - that gave us a third option.

I choked the cow down until she lay on her side with her legs horizontal. Being a good and dutiful wife, Barb came over to pull the rope off for me. But just as she reached down for the rope, the cow came alive!

With a loud bawl, the cow was on her feet in a heartbeat - and Barb was running for the safety of the truck.

It was a wonderful picture! Barb must have jumped a foot in the air! I nearly fell off my horse in a fit of hopeless laughter. But Barb sobered me up in a hurry.

"Get your own damn rope off!" she hollered out the window of the truck, as her spinning wheels threw gravel in my direction.

Diamond D Black

Don had a ranch, but he was not what you would call a cowboy. He had an excellent herd of registered Angus on a well-kept place with lots of irrigation water. The cows were gentle, and the place compact. He had horses, but their job was mainly to pack him into the mountains in the fall.

Don's place was on the flats facing the Rocky Mountain Front in northern Montana. He had a commanding view of the mountains, and of the gap where Birch Creek drains the winter snow-melt out onto the prairie.

During the summer, Don would work hard at his haying. It is a hot and dirty job, and the mosquitoes are always thick around irrigation. But Don could always look up at the mountains and think about the cool, refreshing beauty of the trails and campsites only 25 miles to the West. The high point of his year was the early fall pack - trip which he rarely missed.

One day, Don mentioned to me that he had a horse to break. It was a good big black 3-year-old gelding with Don's Diamond D brand on the left shoulder.

This was my first spring in the Valier area, and I had been helping Don with calving. As the evenings had gotten longer I'd been working on a good corral at my little place up the road. I was finished now, and looking for some horses to work. It didn't take long for us to strike up a deal.

The next evening, Don showed up with his horse in the trailer, along with some hay to feed him for the next thirty days. The horse was gentle, and led nicely to the corral. With the horse taken care of, Don leaned back against the gate and began to tell me the history of the Black.

Don had gotten the colt in trade on some hay. He had been halter-broke and handled some, and he was gentle. A horse doesn't have to be bridle-wise to follow a trail into the mountains, so they had loaded him up along with the others for a pack trip last fall. Don's son was 18 and invincible, so he had volunteered to ride the colt.

When everything was packed up and secure, Mark had swung aboard the Black, and had been promptly and effortlessly thrown to the ground. The speed with which Mark was unseated really shook his confidence. This called for a change of strategy.

They quickly decided that a better way to break the Black to carry weight was to pack him. The horse was plumb gentle and didn't even show much interest as they threw on a pack saddle and piled on a load of unbreakable gear.

They were again ready to hit the trail! But as soon as the lead rope had tightened on the Black he had blown up and scattered his load all through the trees.

Don recounted that they had to tie that pack on three times before they got it tight enough to hold. Finally the colt had given up and consented to carry the load.

It was a beautiful day in a beautiful country. The weight of the work and worry of the past summer had melted off of Don's shoulders as they worked their way into the mountains. The trail followed the creek, and its gurgling coolness helped ease accumulated tensions as the group moved quietly along.

The horses had been pretty subdued when they arrived in camp at the end of the day. They had done very little in the past year besides eat, and they were pretty soft. This was a brand new experience for the black. His body was covered with sweat and his head was hanging a bit as they pulled off the pack saddle. With the horse good and tired like this, it had seemed like a good time for Mark to get on his back again.

But the black was still serious about throwing off his rider. When Mark hit the ground again, they decided to let that aspect of his training wait.

So now it was spring, and they were going to let me take a stab at it. And I, being a real cowboy, was eager to take up the challenge.

After Don left my place, I went into the corral to begin work on the Black. I found him to be as gentle as they said. He led well, he didn't mind a flapping saddle blanket, and he didn't even flinch when I tightened the cinch. There was nothing left to do but climb on.

But again, "discretion is the better part of valor." I know that in the process of evolution, rope was invented before bridles and saddles. And rope is an essential tool for almost everything a cowboy does.

Taking a thick cotton rope, I tied it around the Black's neck. Then I formed a "scotch hobble" by looping it under his rear pastern and tying it off. He was then able to stand on all fours, but he could get no kick with one of his hind legs.

Feeling very secure, I swung aboard. And promptly swung off again as the horse exploded!

I was glad to be clear of him, for he got all tangled up in the rope and went down in pile.

I was really sympathetic to his plight. I talked to him, and rubbed him, and patted him all over. When I was sure that he felt sufficient remorse, I let him up.

The Black was really impressed by my medicine. It took a lot of urging to get him to un-track again with that rope still on him. But we worked through it, and that was the last time he ever tried to buck with me.

I rode the horse for thirty days. We made a few trips over to Don's to let him see our progress. I was proud of how gentle he was, and how well he took a rein. There was no question but what he was cured of his anti-social ideas. So sure was I, that when it came time to send him home, I let my daughter ride him.

Wendy was about 10 at the time, and quite a hand. She had been riding with me wherever I went for the last 5 years. I threw her saddle on and then boosted her two year old brother, Ben, up in front of her. The plan was for them to head over to Don's place, and I would follow with the pickup to get them and their gear.

I puttered around the place for a while and gave them a good lead. Then I jumped in the pickup and followed. They grinned and waved as I passed them on the road. When I looked in the rear view mirror, however, I saw an empty saddle and kids scattered all over the borrow ditch.

The kids weren't hurt, just surprised. I didn't even suspect that the horse had bucked, and I questioned Wendy as to how they had ended up on the ground. She had been trying to get her jacket off, and she had one arm around Ben. I just figured it for some sort of fluke and forgot about it.

A month or so later, Don called. The horse had bucked - really bucked - and Don had dislocated a shoulder in the wreck. Don was really proud of his "beartrap" saddle. It had big sweeping swells that wrapped back over your legs. The thing scared me, and this was the reason why. Rather than being thrown free when the horse started bucking, Don had been held in by those swells. He really took a beating.

I had to protect my reputation, so I rode down and led the horse home. Again I threw on a scotch hobble and swung aboard. But the horse had become a lot more coordinated during his 30 days of riding. This time he didn't get tangled and go down. He bucked! Hard! I stayed aboard - though I would rather not have. If this horse could buck like that with a leg tied, how hard could he buck with it loose?

124

It wasn't long until I could find out. The Birch Creek Rodeo was coming up soon.

Valier is located just off the Blackfoot Reservation. Horses were still a symbol of wealth among the indians and there were hundreds of horses running nearly wild. Every summer, a number of them were gathered for a local show on the edge of the "Rez".

On the appointed day, I loaded the Black into the horse trailer and headed over to the rodeo grounds for an afternoon of beer and horses. I led the horse to the corral as if he were a rope horse rather than a bronc.

But when he came out of the chute, there was no question! With his legs free, and a bucking strap pulled up into his flanks, he really turned the crank. Sonny Campbell won first money on him!

The Black obviously didn't want to be a saddle horse, but he was too big and beautiful to put in a dog food can. I looked at the rodeo schedule.

Cascade was coming up. It was an RCA approved rodeo, with Donny Jacobs as the stock contractor. Jacobs bought canners, but the Black might be more valuable to him as a bucking horse.

When the day came, we again loaded the Black and headed out. Don told me what value he had into the horse, and we agreed to split any profit.

They announced the horse out of the chute as Diamond D. He grunted and kicked and tore up the ground. His rider lasted three jumps. He made good as a bucking horse. After the rodeo, Jacobs wrote out a check for $750.

Now, whenever someone talks about the cruelty of rodeo, I remember the Diamond D Black. He had it made on the lush pastures of Don's Ranch. In return, he had only to pack a rider into the mountains for a couple of weeks out of the year. He had never been beaten; he had never been abused; yet he chose to be an outlaw and to make his living in the rodeo arena.

Fat John

The prairies of Montana, North Dakota, and Alberta are home to numerous colonies of Hutterites. These are a communal Protestant sect of German heritage that engage in agriculture in a big way.

Hutterites are obvious by their dress: the men wear homemade black pants and jackets with bright and gaudy shirts; the women wear long dresses of the same ostentatious colors as the men's shirts, with bright head coverings. They speak German among themselves, and strongly-accented English with outsiders. The surnames among them are fairly limited, with a prevalence of Hofers, Wurz, Wipfs, and Waldners. With a limited number of names to draw from, they often use nicknames.

Hutterites have huge farms, and huge gardens. They often sell their produce at roadside stands, as well as door-to-door. And that's how I met the family of "Crazy Jake" Klinesasser.

One day a pickup drove into the yard and a tall Hutterite man came to the door, stating "I'm J.J.K.K. from the USDA, and I got chickens." He held up some nicely packaged fryers and announced the price.

There are some 50 people in each colony – they eat communally and live in "houses" that may be better described as barracks. Hutterites have the biggest and best farm equipment that money can buy, and their labor costs are minimal. Each colony has wood-working and metal-working shops full of the tools necessary to repair or build anything they use, and they have men with the skill to fabricate most anything.

The Hoots – as they are known locally – are a friendly bunch, and happy to have visitors. One colony was right across the river from my hayground, and one day I stopped by to ask for their help in welding up a piece of equipment.

As I said, their farm equipment is the biggest and best, so their need for labor is minimal – yet they are well-supplied with bodies. Men and boys converged from all sides when I drove up to the shop. The population of that area is pretty sparse, and it was easy enough for them to identify me by the rig I was driving. It wasn't long before someone offered me a beer.

We were discussing what I needed for a repair when a tall Hutterite walked up, thrust his right hand out for a hearty handshake, and reached across with his left to grab my beer and down what remained in the can as fast as he could swallow. The other fellows apologized for his rudeness, and introduced him as "Crazy Jake" – the same "J.J.K.K. from the USDA" that had come to my door a few months back.

I had frequent contact with the men of this colony, as they were an excellent resource. One fellow was a competent – though unlicensed – electrician, and he helped me a few times with my pump. Another fellow was pretty sharp with the wheel lines that irrigated the fields. There were a couple of guys who were master welders, and they had the proper equipment for repairing aluminum pipe. If I needed spare parts for most anything I could borrow from them until I could get to town and secure a replacement. They were good neighbors.

When I needed a tractor driver for a few days I stopped by the colony and they sent over "Fat John", who turned out to be Crazy Jake's son. I put him to discing a field in preparation for re-seeding while I was off shoeing horses for the day. When I came back late in the afternoon I could see that something wasn't right – the tractor was sitting at the far corner of the field at an odd angle. Fat John was nowhere in sight.

Getting closer to the field I could see that John had only made one full round with the tractor, and now I could see that it was stuck. There had been some water leaking out of the ditch and he had bogged the outfit down.

John had learned to drive on a huge four-wheel-drive tractor with dual tires on all four corners. The disc he pulled at the colony was twenty feet wide, had hydraulic cylinders on the wheels to lift it out of the ground, and hydraulics to lift the wings while passing through narrow places. My tractor had only two-wheel-drive, the disc was only ten feet wide, and it had no wheels. To move this disc down a road you had to trip a lever and back up, collapsing the two gangs together to minimize the cutting action of the discs.

When the disc pulled down into the mud John had obviously panicked. With no hydraulic lever to pull to lift the disc out of the ground, the wheels of the tractor had begun to spin.

The first rule of driving in snow or mud is that if your wheels are turning and you're not getting anywhere – SHUT IT OFF!! But for as much expertise as some Hutterites had in other skills, not many of them had the opportunity develop skill as drivers. Whenever they went anywhere their pickup was full of passengers, and only the older of the men had every really done much driving.

With the disc hung up in the mud, John had continued to spin the wheels of the tractor in the vain hope that they would eventually grab and pull the outfit through. Before long, the wheels had dug out all the dirt beneath them, and the tractor was suspended in air – supported by the steering wheels in front and the implement behind.

I don't know when John finally gave up and shut it off, and I don't know how he finally got home – Birch Creek is wide enough and deep enough that I doubt he crossed directly to the colony.

My first task was to detach the disc from the tractor. The hitch was now tight against the ground, and the hitch-pin was in a terrible bind. It took a lot of shoveling, jacking, and hammering to accomplish that. Then I had to extricate the tractor – more shoveling to free the undercarriage and dig ramps for the tires to climb out.

My hay-ground was 15 miles from home, so it was difficult to draft one of the kids to drive the pickup to help pull the tractor out. And at that time – 1985 – I was still driving a two-wheel-drive pickup, which would have been of limited value. Tow-chains were in common usage at the time, rather than the nylon tow-ropes that we use now, which give some elasticity to jerk on a stuck vehicle.

It took awhile to get the tractor out, awhile longer to shovel the dirt back into the trenches that had been dug by the spinning rear tires, and then I had to pull the disc through the wet spot with a chain. It was a few days before I got back to the colony.

"Are you mad Kenny? Are you mad?" asked Fat John when I drove in. He was so innocent and contrite that it was impossible to be angry. And I had met his mother – it was no wonder that John was stupid and his dad – Crazy Jake – was a heavy drinker.

The next time I saw John was in Great Falls nearly ten years later. I was stopped at a light, and watched an excited interchange between him and his mother.

She was yammering in German and gesturing at him as he started into the crosswalk, and he was yammering back and gesturing at her over his shoulder. The fact that they were together on a street corner testified that he was still under her "protective" – and nagging - thumb. But John was actually defying her as he walked ahead across the street.

He'd been so busy arguing with her over his shoulder that he was half-way across the street when he looked up and saw the red light – and quickly scampered back to the corner where his mother stood glaring.

Some things never change.

Fowl Swoop

Horses are endowed with both speed and power, assets that have rendered them invaluable to the purposes of mankind. Man, on the other hand, is so constructed that he walks upright on his hind legs. We humans lack the speed and strength of our four-footed friends, but we enjoy a wonderful amount of mobility and versatility.

Birds have a different combination of characteristics. While they are awkward on land, they have the terrific advantage of flight. Each of God's creatures has its unique place in the world, and each interacts differently within it.

On one particular winter day I was reveling in the respite from the cold which blew in on the wings of a Chinook wind. The snow that had recently covered the broad reaches of the landscape was quickly being driven away, exposing once again the prairie grasses.

In the ranch yard, however, the snow was slower to recede. The steady traffic of both feet and wheels had compressed the fluffy accumulation into a hard crust of ice. The warm wind was able to penetrate only the very surface, leaving on top a thin layer of water. Travel was difficult on this slippery thoroughfare, and fraught with risk.

The chickens were out enjoying this lovely weather, and one chanced to cross the road to see what she might find on the other side. On her return from her exploration, a gust of wind caught the hen off-guard, threatening to topple her over backwards.

In response to this assault on her balance, the chicken spread her wings and gave a quick flap, a reflex meant to return her to an upright position. But she had already been tipped far enough back that her legs were now extended at a 45° angle in front of her. The wet ice offered no traction to her bony feet; she began to slide. The harder the chicken flapped her wings in an attempt to right herself, the faster she slid across the yard.

The wild ride ended with a thud at the chicken house wall, leaving the hen in an undignified heap of wet and ruffled feathers.

After a period of stunned silence, she gathered herself up, checked all over for injuries, and shakily made her way back into the henhouse.

Driver's Education

A well-built fence is a thing of beauty - straight, clean, and symmetrical. There is a simple grace in the long line of evenly spaced and perfectly vertical posts cooperatively bearing the gossamer web of parallel strands of galvanized wire, undulating into the distance, intimately following the curves of "the earth's sweet flowing breast".

It is also a matter of efficiency. A good fence makes a rancher's job easier. And being a lazy man, I'm always in search of the most efficient way to do a job.

Now I _do_ love to ride. When a man's cows are out, or when the neighbor's cows are in, there is riding to do. But there are plenty of other jobs on a ranch that need to be done, and cattle rarely do their straying when it's convenient to gather them up.

Then there is the matter of opening gates. It's always a bother to have to crawl down off your horse, or climb out of your pick-up, to open a pasture gate and shut it again behind you. The job is seriously aggravated by a poorly made brace which requires a person to stretch a half mile of fence in order to get the gate closed again.

The key to a good fence is having solid braces at both ends. In my laziness, I have found it easier to spend the time and effort to build a solid brace in the first place, and avoid years of aggravation.

Behind the artful line of a clean, taut fence is a solid background in science. I got that scientific background during my first year in college.

Physics intrigued me. My interest in the subject led me to doing something I had never done before - homework. I actually read the assigned chapters and arrived in class prepared! It was a new and exhilarating experience. For the first time in my school career I was not afraid to raise my hand to ask a question. I was confident that no one was going to laugh at me - if I didn't know the answer, no one else in the class knew the answer either.

So I took pleasure in my study of physics. I could see the true-life applications of the classroom lessons: levers, gear ratios, hydraulics, transfer of energy, and force vectors.

With this rooted background of understanding, I am well-equipped to quickly appraise the merits of the various brace designs in use on different ranches. My critical study has led me to become very discriminating in my construction practice. (I call it discriminating. Other people speak of my relentless pursuit of perfection in less flattering terms).

I enjoy building fence, and I put my heart in it. I've built miles of new fence, and rebuilt hundreds of miles of old fence. One particular summer, I had found a way to combine two favorite occupations, fencing and riding, into a paying enterprise.

In the late seventies, grain farming had become lucrative. Thousands of acres of prime Montana grazing land had been turned upside down by plows, quadrupling their assessed valuations. On one of these small ranches that had been turned into a large farm overnight, I made a deal with the owner: I would fence the areas that had been too rough to plow, in trade for the right to graze the newly enclosed grass.

This was one of those win/win situations. He would get fences built on his property; I would get free grazing for my small herd of cows. And I was able to sell the excess pasture to a neighbor at a slight profit. This whole package bought me a month of self-employment income - and more excuse to get ahorseback tending to all of the cattle.

The process of building a fence requires trip after trip along the new course. First, the general lay of the fence must be marked and the corner braces set. Then the exact line must be staked over the ridges and down into the coulees. The first strand of wire must be spooled out and stretched tight as a guide for driving the posts. Another trip along the line to lay out posts to be driven a rod (16.5 feet) apart.

My chief helper in this fencing project was my oldest daughter. Amy, 12 that summer, had begun her driving experience years before, steering the pickup away from snow drifts as I flaked the hay out the back.

We'd been working together on the fence for a couple of weeks. It was a hot afternoon and we were both tired, but the end was in sight. The braces were set and the line posts were in. We were spooling out the last three wires from a bar across the back end of the pickup.

The work wasn't going smoothly. The barbs kept snagging on each other and hanging up in the spools. I'd holler for Amy to stop, and then work out the tangle. There were rocks, side-hills, and creeks to navigate. Amy was doing a fine job, and my growing impatience was with the process, not with her.

Near the end of the spools of wire the tangles were worse and more frequent. We'd barely get started when I'd have to shout again for another stop. The fence line came out of a swale and up a little hill. The really difficult factor on this hill was the plow-furrows which crossed our path. The field had been worked up a few years back and seeded to grass, leaving a corrugation which made wheeled travel difficult.

Amy had mastered the three-pedal clutch technique required to start the pickup on a slope, and I was proud of her ability. This is a skill that is only known and appreciated by the select few who use a stick shift vehicle in rugged terrain. With the pickup stopped on a grade, the driver must simultaneously feed throttle with the toe of the right foot, while easing off on the brake pressure with the heel of the same foot, and smoothly engaging the clutch with the left foot. (This maneuver takes about the same level of skill and dexterity required by the executive who carries a briefcase in one hand, and turns the doorknob with the hand holding the cup of coffee.)

There were several other factors which compounded the difficulty of the situation: the two-wheel-drive pickup had no low range, the motor mount was loose, a shock absorber was shot, and Amy was too short to see out over the dash.

Starting the pickup over the furrows caused a lurch that almost threw me out the back, and the wires tangled again. Amy, trying again to ease over a hump, killed the engine a third time. In combination with the hill, the wires, the furrows, and the heat, it was just too much. I let out a shout - and Amy burst into sobs.

We shut off the pickup and quit for awhile. I hugged Amy and reassured her. After the tears were dry I expressed my pride in her: "You've learned more about driving a pickup in one day," I said, "then most people learn in a lifetime".

But to this day she thinks I was hollering at *her*.

Hunter's Education

My son Ben was five years old when I first took him hunting. I was not planning a long drawn-out expedition that would be too much for his little legs - we could find the deer we were after in a hayfield along the creek.

Of course other "great white hunters" would have been after a big buck with an impressive set of antlers. Admittedly, it takes more prowess to get a shot at a critter with a nice rack. But I have always hunted for meat. And as the saying goes, "you can't eat the horns".

For a meat hunter, the sex of a deer is a major consideration. Trophy bucks have more important priorities in the fall than to eat and grow fat. The growth of antlers takes a toll on their bodies, as does the time spent in both fighting and making love. The meat of a buck tends to be tough and stringy, and the taint of their musk-scent is hard to avoid.

The species of deer also affects their suitability for the table. Mule deer tend toward rougher and more sparse areas. Their diets include a courser browse which contributes to a gamier taste. Whitetail are willing to make their homes closer to civilization, and they commonly enjoy the fruits of a farmer's labor.

So, in terms of both time and taste, I was after a whitetail doe. The meat would be tender and mild, and a suitable critter could be found quickly, and close to home.

Ben was still at the stage that he wanted to be just like dad. I would be packing a rifle, and so must he. So I fashioned him one out of the materials at hand. From a 1X4 pine board I cut out the shape of a rifle stock. A length of broom handle made the barrel. We dug out an old hunters orange vest, and we were ready!

At daylight the next morning we headed out. It was only half a mile to Dupuyer Creek where we would find ideal conditions for whitetail, and Ben was an eager companion.

My deer hunting technique is unsophisticated. I simply move slowly along the brushy creek bottom until I find my quarry. Ben followed along at my flank, senses alert and "rifle" at ready.

The sun was barely up when we sighted a deer headed back to the safety of the brush after a night spent grazing on alfalfa. This was a single doe, surely without young; a prime candidate for our freezer.

The eyes of the hunter and the hunted met simultaneously, and we all froze in place while we assessed the situation, about 40 yards between us. The deer was still undecided as to what danger we humans posed when my rifle barked.

I heard the satisfying "Thwaack" of bullet meeting flesh, but the deer did not go down. A sick feeling of disgust filled my belly as the animal broke into a run for the creek, dragging an injured hind leg.

Modern firearms pack a terrific wallop. Precision bullets, metered charges, and telescopic sights give latter day hunters every advantage. But even the best of equipment cannot guarantee accuracy over human error.

Each fall there are a significant number of game animals that die a slow death after such crippling shots as I had just delivered. Sometimes the range is too great; sometimes an animal moves at a critical moment. "Buck fever" is undoubtedly a factor in a majority of cases.

I had seldom needed a second bullet to knock down an animal. But today, right in front of my impressionable young son,

I had blown the leg off a deer! This unmitigated embarrassment was to be his introduction to hunting - a lesson he would carry for the rest of his life.

It took only seconds for the injured deer to cover the 40 yards to a fence where it effortlessly cleared the top wire. But instead of disappearing into the brush along the creek, the animal merely piled up in a heap on the other side!

Ben and I headed for the fence at a run. There was no sign of life as we approached the deer. Keeping an eye on the inert form, we helped each other between the wires.

As Ben looked on, I drew my knife and began to dress out the deer, giving him an impromptu lesson in anatomy. Opening up the chest cavity we found massive destruction. The path of the bullet was obvious - dead center through the chest, destroying the heart. It was the exit through the off-side shoulder that had caused the deer to run with a distinct limp.

What had appeared, for a short time, to be an awful example of careless marksmanship turned out to be an excellent lesson for a young hunter: about the hunting prowess of his father and the ability of an animal to function long after it is dead.

The Palomino Filly
and the
Mammoth Jack

The little place that we had rented southwest of Valier was just a few acres with a house and a barn, and it was surrounded by irrigated farm ground. During the winter there was plenty of room to ride in the neighboring fields. But once the crops were seeded, my world closed in and the riding space was severely limited.

The whole situation was too much like what I had seen on the Fairfield Bench and I wasn't too excited. But I'd found a decent calving job, and green horses were abundant in the area. Rent was fair, the school bus went by the door, and I couldn't afford to be choosy. It didn't take long to fill my corrals, and I had 6-8 horses at a time to break.

The deal I was making on most of these horses was to ride them for thirty days. At the end of that time I guaranteed them to "neck-rein in a halter bareback". Wendy was the final test before I sent the horse home: if she could guide them around the place with only a lead rope, they were "done".

The first week with a new horse is all corral work. I used my vast arsenal of ropes, hobbles, saddles, bridles, straps, and gunny sacks to convince a horse that I wasn't mean, but that I *was* in charge, and that he would do as I asked. When the trainee was sufficiently compliant to my requests on the reins, it was time to climb aboard.

I've been riding for as long as I remember, and my childhood riding was mostly bareback. I am completely comfortable on a horse's back and have excellent balance. Staying in the middle of a horse that has "broke in two" is an exhilarating experience. I love the challenge of making a good horse.

But the earth doesn't give much when you fall from 5 feet up, and a broken arm takes about 6 weeks to heal. To climb on the back of a horse which is scared and/or angry, and which you know is going to buck, always seemed foolish to me. By doing the appropriate groundwork first, I generally avoid the storm that many people expect on the first rides.

After a few days of starting, stopping, and reining around the corral, a horse and rider both get bored and it is time to head out and see a little country. One day I would work a horse on reining around through the shelter belt. The next day we would head out at a long trot looking for ditches and tractors and swamps and whatever new experiences we could find.

As I said, my routes were somewhat limited by growing crops in the summer. Behind the house was an access road heading west a few miles where it ran past a field of irrigated pasture. From there I could pick my way across and cut through a forty-acre field of improved pasture which belonged to John Holden. John's gate opened onto the gravel county road that led out to the oiled main road.

I frequently rode through that forty of John's. It was a handy little field for him, and he used it for whatever odd livestock that needed a temporary home. One day there'd be a late-calving cow; the next time I came through there might be a lame bull.

On this particular day I was riding a little palomino filly who was sweet, docile, and gentle. She was eager to please and had never offered to buck. We were half way across John's little field when the filly stopped dead in her tracks, nearly throwing me over her head. I followed her gaze toward the far corner. Just visible over a little rise in the ground was a pair of long ears headed our way.

The little horse stood spraddle-legged and trembling as those flopping appendages grew bigger. We still weren't quite sure to what they were attached. Then we heard a brassy and mournful Heeeeeeeeeeeeee-Haaaaaaaaaaaaaaaaaaaw as the head of John's mammoth jack appeared.

Mules are made by breeding donkeys to mares. To get a nice-sized mule you need a good tall jack. John had kept this big jack at stud during the breeding season that had just ended.

The filly quickly decided that "discretion is the better part of valor" and started leaving as fast as she had stopped going, and she almost lost me again as she bolted.

We were traveling as fast as the filly's pounding hooves could carry us. A jack-leg fence was two hundred yards away and coming closer by the second. I could picture in my mind the wreck that was about to happen: when we hit that fence it would roll with us, and I would be entangled in a razor-sharp web along with a franticly struggling horse.

It seemed to me a good idea to get off <u>before</u> the wreck. But looking down, I could see all the sharp little rocks that had been pulled to the surface when the field had been worked up and seeded to grass. At the speed we were going, I knew that skidding across those rocks was really going to hurt.

Luckily, the filly began to weaken. And when the donkey topped the rise, the palomino could see that - although the approaching monster was different than her -, it was <u>some</u> sort of equine. I took advantage of her hesitation and circled her away from the fence and straight toward the gate. I had no more faith in the intentions of that lonely and love-starved donkey than did my horse, and we were both eager to be away from there.

Pulling down my lariat, I used it to keep the donkey at bay until we could get through the gate. The horse and I were both dripping sweat as we headed back down the road from whence we came. I felt lucky to get out of that field with all of my skin intact, and I vowed that in the future I would always scout the occupants of that field before I ventured through.

Afoot!

A cowboy is just another farmer when he is afoot, and I wasn't happy when it happened to me one spring day. My calving job with the neighbors was finished and I now was working on a pen full of green horses.

Ten head in training is a full time job. My strategy is to spend some time with each horse every day. During the second week with a horse, he is ready to ride outside the pen. My goal is to give each horse alternate lessons - one day a shorter session around the barn fine-tuning his handling, and the following day a good long trot to burn off stress and "see some country".

This particular day I was riding through a pasture on a blue roan belonging to Don Rose when I came to an irrigation ditch with a scant amount of water. We found a shallow crossing, and the roan hesitated only slightly before stepping across. Our tour was uneventful and we were heading back to the barn with a good wet saddle blanket when we returned by way of the ditch.

This time the roan pulled up short. He snorted at the water and whirled around to avoid the paltry stream.

Of course there was no question about whether he would cross. I turned him back around to face the water - and he whirled the other way. As I got more aggressive with the colt, he only became more stubborn.

I tried coaxing, and I tried demanding. I kicked with my heels and I slapped with the reins. I approached straight on, and angled from different directions. I rode along the edge of the water as the bank became steeper, trying to force the horse across. I was mad, I was humiliated, and I was getting tired. But I was making no progress.

I kept my eyes peeled for any sign of a witness to my plight, but so far my failure had not been exposed. Finally I gave it up. Tying the horse to a fence post, I *walked* back to the barn, careful not to be seen by any neighbors. I caught and saddled a broke horse, found an old lariat to use as a war bridle, and headed back out.

A war bridle is a halter affair fashioned from a lariat. It has the capacity to inflict a brutal amount of pain on a horse that chooses not to give to a gentle pull on the rope. Used on a green or scared horse it can be very counter-productive, blinding him with pain and giving him a life-long fear of a lead-rope. But used properly on a halter-broke horse, it can remind him gently – or not so gently – that he is to give to the pull.

Rigging the war bridle on the roan, we rode around the field looking for places the horse didn't care to travel. Whenever he hesitated, the rope tightened on his head. When he acknowledged my power by slacking the rope, I gave him love and sympathy, and loosened the rigging on his head. After the short training session, we were ready to tackle the crossing again.

A horse laying back on a rope has a lot more weight and power advantage than the lead horse with the rope dallied to the horn, so I hit the ditch at an angle. When the roan set his feet, I turned off and pulled from an angle preventing him from bracing against the pull. He gave to the rope – and cleared the ditch by six feet!

We turned around and crossed the ditch again. This time he jumped five feet; then four feet; then three; then two. As the roan gathered himself for the next pass across, I turned my horse off. While the black's feet were still in the air I pulled him back around and dropped him right in the ditch.

As he stood there in the cool water, sides heaving and sweat dripping, I gave him more sympathy. Then I led him up and down the ditch, crossing and re-crossing on a slack lead.

Finally I tied up my broke horse and rode the roan through the water a few more times, reassured that I was indeed smarter than a horse.

Christmas Eve

I'd been living outside of Valier for a few years, doing whatever I could to make a living: training horses, helping a neighbor during calving, contracting fence, summering cows, cooking for an outfitter in the Bob Marshall Wilderness, putting up hay, shoeing horses... But winter was always slow for paying work. One day I answered an ad for a UPS driver, and got hired for the Christmas season.

It wasn't a job I enjoyed. You are alone in the truck, but the management keeps track of how many miles you drive, how many stops you make, how many packages you deliver, and how long it takes you to complete your route. If anything interrupts the flow of your day it will show up in your stats, and you are sure to hear about it from your supervisor the next day.

These UPS vans are designed for city use, rather than the open spaces of Montana. They are cold, and they are helpless in snow.

On one particular day it was relatively warm, so there was a layer of water on top of the slowly melting snowpack that was present in every farmyard in the region. I had to be careful where I parked the van to deliver a package, because I had almost no traction when I started out again. Nearly every stop was followed by a drawn-out series of attempts to go forward or reverse before I finally arrived back on the highway.

Back at the barn the next morning my supervisor cornered me before I could leave with the truck:

"What happened yesterday? You were two hours over!"

"I was stuck", says I.

151

"How long did it take for you to get out? Fifteen minutes; twenty minutes?"

"I was stuck all day," I said. "Every time I stopped it took a few minutes to get going again."

The supervisor went off grumbling, but at least he had served notice that he was watching. I had a set of tire chains, but I would have had to put them on to go up each of 20 driveways, and take them off again every time I returned to the highway.

But the worst part about the job was the uniform. I was delivering a rural route in country with which I was reasonably familiar, in a place where people knew me in my "civilian" life. I was a cowboy, and I was embarrassed to have people see me in such a get-up as I was required to wear by UPS – as embarrassed as I would have been for people to see me afoot out on the prairie.

It paid well, however, at time of the year when pickin's were slim. And besides, it was only a temporary job.

The last week before Christmas is always frantic with the UPS and USPS, right up through Christmas Eve – and that's why they hired a few extra drivers. But then the job was over. This particular Christmas Eve had been especially bad, with a truck-load of packages and a snow-storm building out of the northwest. I was looking forward to joining my family, snug around a roaring fire. I parked my truck, punched the time-clock for the last time, and headed out the door into the darkness.

The car I was driving that night came with its own story: I had broke two Arabian horses for a gal in trade for a third one. I broke the three together, and traded my horse out of the deal to another guy for an Audi Fox. It was one of the early front-wheel-drive outfits, and I felt as silly driving it as I did wearing the UPS uniform.

But the UPS center was in Cut Bank – 30 miles north of Valier. The Audi burned a lot less gas than the suburban, and was the reasonable choice for commuting. It was small, but there was enough room in the back seat for a scoop shovel and the bag of winter clothes that I carried with me on the UPS truck.

I left Cut Bank headed for home. My hitch with UPS finished, and I was facing a whole week of freedom!

But there was a barricade across the road at the Valier junction, and a highway patrolman to inform me that the road was closed.

It would be a 100-mile detour around through Shelby and down, and the same storm was blowing there. I was tired, hungry, and impatient.

"The road is closed due to blowing and drifting snow," said the patrolman, who like me, wanted to be home with his family.

"I'm going home," I told him. "I have a front-wheel-drive outfit, plenty of clothes, and a scoop shovel. I'm not going to spend the holidays in Cut Bank."

"The worst that can happen," I told him, "is that I have to turn around and come back. With that he let me go on.

There was indeed snow driving in from the west, and visibility was poor. Headlights only lit up the snow swirling in the air, and did little to illuminate the road. I was in big farm country, and residences were few and far between. At least there were no headlights coming at me to make it harder to see.

Finger drifts were growing along the right side of the road, but there was no traffic to prevent me from using the left side. Occasionally, however, blasting through those drifts sent my car into a swerve.

Before long I approached a drift that was too big to attempt. I got out my scoop and began to dig a path through it. But the snow was heavy, and the wind was filling in behind me faster than I could dig ahead. On the other side of the drift was a set of headlights.

Giving up my attempt to dig through, I walked across the drift to confer with the driver on the other side. It was a pickup driven by my insurance agent from Valier, heading to Cut Bank for the company Christmas party.

We agreed that this drift was the end of the line for both of us. He would return to Valier - and yes, he had room for me in the pickup.

I went back to my car and drove it to downwind side of the road so the drift it made would be into the borrow-ditch. The agent drove me on out to my house - and I DID get to spend Christmas with my family.

Extreme Weather

In March of 1986 I got a phone call that put the smile back on my face. The fellow who had been the "straw boss" at the Blacktail Ranch had taken a town job. Calving was in full swing and a replacement was needed immediately.

My main source of revenue at the time was my haying operation. It was a 320 acre lease along Birch creek where I put up 800 to 1,000 tons of hay during the summer. It kept me busy from May through August, but it didn't make enough money to keep me through the rest of the year.

I'd spent the last three calving seasons working for my neighbor, Don, who raised purebred angus bulls. Don was easy to work for, but all his calving was done in corrals. He had horses, but they were only used for his pack trips into the Rocky Mountains, 30 miles west.

The Blacktail was a "real" ranch. There were 800 cows to care for and only two men to do it. There was a minimum of corrals and a maximum of horse-work.

I called Gene, who had a contract to manage the place, and offered my services. He'd had me in mind, he said, and we quickly made a deal.

Mike's new job started on April first. On the day before, his pickup and mine crossed paths continually as I moved my family in and he moved his family out.

The weather was cooperative for this change in command. It had been beautiful spring weather for a week now, and a pleasant Chinook wind was blowing. Jim was doing the feeding, and the cows didn't require immediate attention.

It was dark when the moving was finished, and I was thankful for a shower and bed. I wasn't acquainted with this particular ranch, but I was eager to jump back into the familiar work of calving a big bunch of cows on the prairie.

As usual, I awoke early. The sky was bright at 6:00 and I dressed quickly. There was no provision on this ranch for checking the cows at night - I would be making a check of the cattle every morning at first light.

But the sight that met my eyes on this first morning set me back on my haunches. The normally inconsequential Blacktail Creek that lay between the house and the barn was today in raging flood!

There was a good snowpack in the Rockies this spring, and the warm Chinook wind had started a good share of it toward the ocean. Blacktail had been only a few feet wide yesterday, and had meandered harmlessly under the bridge. This morning the bridge was submerged, and the water spread out over several acres in front of me.

In the garage, I dug through boxes until I found my hip boots. I hadn't expected to use them for another month or two when I started to irrigate the hay.

The narrow foot-bridge across the creek to the barn had only the handrails visible. Cattle and horses were standing knee-deep in the water in the corrals.

Sam nickered as he saw me coming; his breakfast lay submerged and soggy. The plank floor in the barn was high enough that Sam could get out of the water, and I let him eat dry hay while I threw on the saddle.

The first order of business was to open the corral gates and let the few enclosed cattle out to higher ground. Then Sam and I set out to survey the situation.

I really had no understanding of the terrain past what I could surmise from protruding objects. I didn't know what classes of livestock were in which fields, nor even where the fields lay. I pointed the horse out toward what I assumed to be the "heavy" bunch and gave him his head.

Sam and I had covered a lot of miles together, and he was a good steady mount, but he had never impressed me with his athletic ability. I don't know if he was really clumsy, or if it was just a ruse to get him out of work. Over the years he had fallen with me several times, and I didn't trust his sense of balance. However, the other two horses I had brought with me to the ranch were both green, and I this wasn't the ideal time for training.

The barn and corrals had been built in the trees along the creek. Ordinarily, it was a good spot to be - protected as it was from the wind. But hidden by the floodwaters were branches, rocks, and old creek channels.

The cattle in this calving field were bunched at the far fence, higher up and out of the water. Sam stumbled a few times, and found a few holes to step down into as we headed up onto dry ground. We rode slowly through the bunch and everything there seemed to be fine.

My hired man, Jim, lived in Dupuyer and drove out every day. He had worked on the place for a couple of years and could tell me more about the layout. I went back to the house to have breakfast and wait for him.

When Jim arrived, he stopped on the far side of the water. We hollered and waved back and forth, and I signaled him to wait there.

I went back to the barn and climbed on Sam. We waded through the water with a little more assurance this time, and

157

circled around to where Jim stood. I gave him a hand up behind me and we rode double back to the barn.

The water around the barn was past overboot high. Jim had no hip boots, so I gave him a piggy-back ride across the footbridge to higher ground, then set off on Sam to check the heavies again while Jim loaded the wagon to feed. Returning with the tractor, he halted in the yard. We would have to cross the submerged bridge with the outfit in order to feed.

With a pole in my hand and my boots well up past my knees, I started in the general direction of the bridge, feeling my way through the water. Before I reached the bridge, the water was lapping at my boot-tops.

It would be foolish to drive through the water without landmarks. If the tractor were to hit the bridge off-center we could loose the whole works. We began to sort out options.

I hated to let the livestock go all day without feed. But the weather was nice and the risk of crossing the creek was too high. Jim and I had to content ourselves with riding among the cattle and making sure all the calves were mothered up and out of danger.

By the next day, the creek was down enough that we were able to find the bridge. We held our breaths as Jim inched across, trusting that the flooding hadn't washed out the piles holding the bridge up.

The warm weather continued and the ranch dried out. We resumed the routine of calving. Mornings found us feeding cattle, and afternoons we spent ahorseback. The weather treated us well, and life was good.

The morning of April 20, I had to look twice at the thermometer. I always checked the temperature before I dressed to determine how much clothes I needed. Ten degrees above zero would have been a little chilly for this time of year, but the thermometer said ten *below!*

I had been living in Montana for most of twenty years by then, and I was rarely surprised by the weather. It is not unusual to see a change of 50° in a matter of a few hours, and it can snow any month of the year. But this was the height of calving, and a new wet calf doesn't last long at that temperature.

My wool underwear had been washed and put away until next fall, but I dug them out again. Likewise, I had to look around for my mitts.

Outside, it was clear and cold. I quickly saddled a horse and rode into the calving field.

It was easy to spot one new arrival. The wobbly calf was nosing up to his mother's warm udder for his first meal. The cow had done a good job of licking him off, but the calf was still damp. Dropping down from the horse, I felt his ears. They were already hard.

Packing a calf on a horse is awkward at best. First you have to get a grip on his slippery hide, then throw him up across the saddle. If your horse hasn't yet shied or bucked, you can swing up behind the calf and start for the barn.

But the ride is uncomfortable for both man and beast, and it's usually not long before the calf starts to scramble. Even a broke horse can get hard to control with a calf floundering across his back.

Usually the cow will began to bawl and sniff the ground where she last saw her calf. She might have seen him thrown onto the horse, and sometimes she'll follow for a few steps. But the cow will nearly always go back to where you picked up the calf.

The Blacktail ranch was over-stocked with 800 cows. It had a hay base for about 350, and the facilities were not set up for so many animals. The calving shed was well designed, but it had only seven pens.

I dropped the new calf in the barn and went back after his mother. She was still bawling frantically and searching the area where the odor of her calf was still evident.

The cow kept trying to dodge back to the spot she had lost her calf, but my horse and I were up to the game. After several attempts to get past us, the cow finally lined out toward the barn.

Inside, there was a happy reunion. The calf soon found a faucet, and the pair was content.

Returning to the field, I saw a cow in active labor. She would wander along the fence restlessly, occasionally stopping with her tail straight out, straining to expel a calf.

We pulled in behind the cow and took her back down the fence to the barn. It took a couple of passes for her to find the door, but the gates inside were already set to run her into the next pen.

Leaving her to her business, I headed back out into the cold and promptly found another new calf, humped up and shivering.

Before long I had two new pairs in the barn, and two that were calving. Things seemed to have quieted down for a bit, so I went in for breakfast.

When Jim arrived at 8:00 I was back out ahorseback. The low barometric pressure in advance of a storm will often cause a flurry of births among the cows that are near term. This arctic blast had come in so fast that even the cows were caught by surprise - all of them seemed to be calving at once.

I enlisted Jim's aid bringing in calves with the pickup. Our seven pens were soon full. With more new calves coming, we needed space in the barn. Two that were warm, dry, and full of milk went back outside with their mothers, and two more cows were brought in to calve.

The air in the barn was humid from the concentration of animals. When I rode in, the moisture immediately condensed on the frozen surface of my glasses leaving me temporarily blind.

In the clear blue sky the sun shone brightly as the morning progressed. The strength of its rays increased as it rose higher, and the frost began to disappear from the course hair of the cattle. Jim went off to feed while I hurried the cows in and out of the shed as they calved and mothered up.

By mid afternoon the thermometer had risen to 20° and the pace of calving had slackened. It was no longer necessary to bring in a new calf if he got up and began to suck soon after birth.

The pens in the barn were still full at dark - there were a few calves that had been slow to get started. But the danger was past. We had 32 calves born in that one 24-hour period, *and we had saved every one!*

Mad Cow

During calving time on the Blacktail Ranch west of Valier I had primary responsibility for the cattle work. I spent most of the day ahorseback, checking on the cattle and taking care of any problems.

One afternoon I had in the corral a cow and her new calf who was not doing well. The calf was slow to nurse, and I was giving him a bottle to get him off to a good start. My horse was tied to the fence by the gate where I had brought the pair in.

My son was 5 years old, and took the bus to Kindergarten every other day. After school he found me at the barn. Ben had been raised on a ranch and often helped me with the cattle. We would figure on saddling his horse now that he was home from school.

He crawled between the fence poles and was walking across the corral to join me when the cow took offense. She caught Ben with her head and pinned him up against the barn wall.

Her head was nearly as big as he was, and it weighed more! As she bellowed and worked him over, the only thing that kept him from being crushed was her stub horns.

The majority of beef cattle are bred to be polled - that is hornless. Most of the remaining cattle have their horn-buds removed at branding to prevent any growth. This cow, however, had a short pair of horns that just fit around a little boy and transferred to the barn the brunt of her force.

I sprang to his aid as quickly as possible and drove the cow away. But not before she had skinned him up, bruised him, and scared a few days off the end of his life. Had a horn hooked the middle of his chest rather than straddling him, he likely would have been killed.

The next summer my family made a trip that took us through Yellowstone Park. We found ourselves in a long line of cars moving very slowly down the road. As we moved up the way we discovered the cause of the delay - a buffalo cow and calf were in the field close to the road.

The whole family was amazed to see the tourists out of their cars and moving in for picture of the wild pair. Ben could easily have been killed by the protective response of a domestic cow, and these idiots were trying to get close to a wild buffalo!

Cricket

I had picked up a stocky little gray to fill an order for a buggy horse. He was green, but had seemed pretty quiet, and he had come cheap. I got him home and began to break him.

Most ranch-raised horses are pretty spooky until they get used to people, but this one never settled down. It didn't take long to figure out that this horse was not the kind to plug along in front of buggy.

I put a lot of riding on him in attempt to make a marketable horse. But he was no fun to ride - he wasn't interested in cattle, and he wasn't an athlete. He was slow, he stumbled a lot, and the spook didn't work out of him. He was literally afraid of his own shadow.

With all the riding, the Gray was gentle enough. But you just never knew when he might shy back or jump sideways. I figured his eyes must be bad.

I wanted to sell him, but I didn't know who I could find to buy him. It took a cowboy to ride the flighty bugger, but a cowboy wouldn't want him. He just wasn't much; not for looks, not for personality, not for ability. The only thing the Gray could do well was pace - travel in a smooth 2-beat gait in which both legs on the same side travel the same direction at the same time. Most horses trot - a gait in which the legs on opposite corners travel together. A horse can trot all day and cover a lot of ground, but it takes effort on the part of the rider to sit that gait.

Grandpa Hanawalt had been a Tennessee Walker breeder. He bragged on how nice it was to ride their pacing gait. "Just like riding in a rocking chair," he used to say. In fact, that breed is also known as a "Plantation Walking Horse", and was developed for 'Massa' to have a smooth ride while he was out checking on the slaves. Maybe that worked in Tennessee, but I wanted a horse that was quick and sure-footed.

I was complaining one day to Merle Tatsey. Merle is a Blackfoot Indian who was working for the irrigation project that brought the water to my hay fields. When I mentioned that the horse could pace, Merle's ears perked up. "Don't show him to me," says Merle.

"Why not?" I asked.

"Because I always wanted a horse that could pace," replied Merle.

Horses are still considered a measure of wealth on the Blackfoot Reservation. And Merle kept his share of the "shitters". I had found the man who wanted this horse and wouldn't be afraid of his flighty nature.

The first chance I got, I jumped the Gray into the back of the pickup and headed up the creek to Merle's place. Unloading the horse, I flipped up on the gray bareback and strutted around the field using only the halter to guide him. The graceful smooth stride quickly had Merle hooked.

"The only horse I've got to trade is a big 3-year-old that Walt is riding for me," says he.

"It's a trade," says I, and left before Merle could change his mind.

It was a couple of weeks before Merle showed up with my new horse. He turned out to be a great big beautiful sorrel gelding! I was sure pleased with his looks and I was eager to find out what this horse was like to ride.

When I got aboard him, however, I was not so sure I had gotten the best of the deal. The horse had that unmistakable feel of tension that precedes a blow-up. I was a long way off the ground, and this horse was about to buck!

I was in the middle of haying and didn't have the time, the facilities, nor the inclination to mess with him then. I bailed off before he decided to "break in two".

My hay-ground was about 15 miles from home, so I had set up a trailer to stay during haying season. Using horses to get around when I was irrigating saved me a lot of walking, and was darn good training for young horses. We had thrown up a temporary corral at the hay camp and I quickly put the sorrel in with the others.

After supper, I sent Wendy out to lead all the horses down to water from the creek. She came running back breathlessly, yelling that the Sorrel had jumped the fence and was headed north.

I tried to get around him with the pickup, but I didn't want to track up the hay, or drive into an irrigation ditch. He got past us, and out the open gate. I was too busy with the haying to spend time chasing horses. He couldn't go far anyway. In a few days I would have time to look, and I expected to find him in a fence corner somewhere, near some other horses.

The Reservation is not a good place to lose a horse. There are hundreds of them running loose, and fences are not very well kept. I had been missing another horse for more than a year. When I finally got the time to go looking for the Sorrel, I was disappointed to find that he had completely quit the country.

It was in the Fall a year later when Gene Curry rode into the yard on his "iron horse." He had been out on the "Rez" looking for some of *his* horses, and he came in with an interesting story.

He told of spotting two of his mares in a fence corner, with a third horse. On his way toward them, he had dropped into a coulee out of sight. When he got up to where he could see them again, the third horse was on the other side of the fence. If he had seen right, he said, that horse would have had to flat-footed jump that 4-wire fence!

"Was he a tall, good-looking sorrel," I asked?

167

"Yes he was," replied Gene.

"That's *my* horse," I exclaimed!

We saddled up and headed over north to bring the horses in. It didn't take too much maneuvering to throw the Sorrel in with the mares and run them all back to the ranch.

On the way in, I looked this sorrel over to make a positive identification. After all, I'd only seen the horse once, a year ago, and for only a few minutes. I hadn't gotten a brand inspection then, and didn't even know what brand he should have.

It took several phone calls to learn about the background of the Sorrel and to be satisfied he was mine. Turk Cobell had bred him, but had traded him off as a colt. He was of racing bloodlines, half Quarter Horse and half Thoroughbred

The horse had passed through several hands before Merle got a hold of him as a 3-year-old. The Sorrel had Turk's brand on him, and so I got a bill of sale from Turk. He had already jumped over two fences, so I named him Cricket.

Now that I had him home in a good stout corral, it was time to see what kind of horse he was.

Cricket was plainly not gentle broke. He hadn't been when I'd first been on him, and now he'd been running out on the rez' for another a year. I've never made any claims about being a bronc rider. My method is to work *with* a horse, and try to avoid fireworks. Pride didn't keep me from doing some groundwork on this horse to settle him down a bit before I got on his back again.

After a few sessions in the corral afoot, there was nothing else to do; I had to ride him. I climbed aboard, screwed myself down tight, and squeezed. Sure enough, the sorrel broke in two.

He didn't buck long, and he didn't buck hard, and I was still aboard when he quit. I had to grin about the whole deal. I just might have myself a keeper!

I rode Cricket a lot that winter. He got to be real gentle. By calving time in the spring, I was sure enough a horseback! Cricket really took to the cows and was a natural cutting horse. At better than 16 hands and over 1200 pounds, he was big enough to work a rope.

And he knew how to handle his feet! At any speed, on any terrain, in any weather, I could count on him to stay under me, and upright. On one particular occasion, we were fast and hard after some dry cows that were trying to make their escape. We were going flat-out across the prairie when we hit a badger patch.

With holes all around us, it would have been easy for him to trip, fall, or break a leg, and we were in the middle of them before we had time to stop. There was nothing I could do except stay out of the way and not throw Cricket off balance. I pitched him the reins and sat up straight in the saddle.

I know that all of his feet didn't touch down in cadence as we flew through! He seemed to just skip a step when there was a hole underneath, and take two, somehow, when he found solid ground.

Emerging from the riddled knob in one piece, Cricket again poured on the coal and we soon had the cows put where we wanted them to be.

Although he was an excellent horse, he did have one annoying habit: every morning he bucked - not long, and not hard, but *every* morning. Most days, with a little patience, I could have talked him out of his bucking. But he wasn't serious, and we both enjoyed it.

He and I impressed some of the neighbors. They figured that if I could ride a great big mean horse like Cricket, I could sure enough ride. And I never saw a reason to spoil that illusion.

As long as I stayed on that ranch, Cricket was my buddy. We covered many miles together and he got me out of lots of real tight situations. No horse is perfect. But for the work I had, Cricket was close enough.

Vinegar Pie

By necessity, most ranches are a long way from town. It takes thousands of acres of grass to feed enough cows to support a family, and only a few of those large acreages can be the ones that are close in. Most of the country roads are gravel – dusty in the summer, icy in the winter, and rutted in the spring.

Another fact of ranch life is that weekends rarely mean two days off for recreation. Work days are usually as long as the daylight allows, and the cows have to be fed seven days a week for months on end.

This combination of poor roads, long distance, and limited time sure cuts down on trips to town. For years my family bought most of the month's groceries in the one big trip to town when I got paid at the end of the month. With 5 kids to feed and clothe, we didn't spend money on such extravagances as cold cereal, pop-tarts, or soda. We bought most food in as basic a form as possible – both to save money, and to save cupboard space. That meant grinding wheat into cracked wheat cereal, or into flour. For years, sour-dough whole wheat buns and fry-bread were staples in our diet.

Fresh, hot fry-bread is food of the gods! With lots of butter, and jam or honey, a fellow can eat until he's ready to burst for mere pennies worth of wheat. Likewise cracked wheat cereal with honey and heavy cream makes a tasty and economical breakfast – especially when combined with a patty of sausage.

And we made an ice cream desert – "chocolate bombe" it was called in the cookbook – by folding a cocoa solution into whipped cream that was only hours away from our own cow. On occasion I would mix up some baking cocoa with butter, powdered sugar, and coconut to make something like a Mounds candy.

But sometimes a fellow would develop a longing for something different to titillate his taste buds. There was no coffee shop with fresh pastries within two hours drive, and we could afford neither the gas nor the price of the goodies.

One winter's evening I was overcome by the desire for something sweet. Paging through the cookbook I saw lots of recipes for desserts that would satisfy my craving, but one after another required an ingredient we didn't have on hand.

Finally I came to a recipe for vinegar pie. Flour, sugar, oil, vinegar, cloves – we had them all! It was hard to imagine that a pie made from vinegar could be tasty, but it was described as resembling lemon pie. So I made it.

The finished product didn't look any more appealing than it sounded. The pie was kind of a mud-colored custard, tinted by the spices that gave it flavor. But I was desperate, and I had to at least *taste* it.

It was good! It did taste like lemon pie – at least to someone who hadn't seen a lemon for months – and through the years it became sort of family trademark.

Soap Hole!

It was already a beautiful summer day, but it was made better by the job that was ahead of us. Thaine Wulff, owner of the Blacktail Ranch on which we lived, had called and asked for a load of dry cows.

The ranch was located about 15 miles west of Valier, on the southeast corner of the Blackfeet Reservation. Thaine himself lived in Great Falls and ran the Sun River Cattle Company, a large feedlot where he fattened calves. My job was to care for the brood cows and deliver the calves to him in the fall.

I had calved around 800 head for him that spring. The place was a good hay-base, but hadn't enough pasture to summer the cows. Nearly all the pairs had been trucked away in May to pasture until fall in another part of "the Rez". All that were left on the ranch were assorted cripples, late calvers, and drys.

The facilities of the ranch were not designed for intensive management, so most of the cows calved out on pasture during the spring. We'd done a good job with them, however, and had lost only 38 calves - 95% calving percentage.

The pairs had all gone off the ranch to pasture, leaving only these dry cows at home. In addition to the cows that had lost their calves were a few open cows that had either slipped past the pregnancy tester or had lost their calves earlier in their pregnancies. These cows were all over north in the Alkali Lake field.

Summer on a ranch is mostly dedicated to the task of putting up the winter's feed. Haying is a hot, dusty, greasy, noisy job. And it isn't horseback. We were glad for the chance to fork our horses and log a little time on their backs.

A bonus of this job was that the cows we were after were dry - they had no calves. Fat and sassy and unfettered by responsibility to their offspring, these girls would be likely to run in every direction, giving us an excuse to use our horses to capacity. In short, a COWBOY job!

Wendy was 13 at the time, and my main helper in anything that had to do with horses. She was riding a full-blood Arab that she was breaking for Phil Michaels who ranched north of Cut Bank. I was riding my buddy, Cricket.

We squeezed our horses into a trot as we covered the 3 miles of prairie between us and the field that held the cows. We needed 53 cows to fill the possum-belly stock truck that would arrive shortly after noon.

On our approach, the drys sorted themselves away from the odd few pairs that were in the pasture. They were obvious as they put their heads and tails in the air and headed away at a brisk pace. We kept up our long trot while hazing them in the general direction of the fence corner where we would make the final cut.

Wendy and I were spread out amongst the scattered cows, drifting our gather toward the southwest. Most of the drys moved off in the appropriate direction, gathering with the others that we had started. There was one old girl, however, who had other ideas. She liked the freedom of the range and was sure we had nothing better in store for her.

With a grin on my face I busted Cricket out after her and gave chase. We were just about up to where we could head her when we found ourselves in the middle of a badger flat.

Badgers are common in that area. In fact Blacktail Creek runs into a creek named Badger just a few miles below the ranch. These reputedly mean carnivores prey on the gophers (Richardson Ground Squirrels) which over-populate most of central Montana. The gophers are nuisance enough, but the holes that the badgers leave, digging after their quarry, are a danger to both man and equipment.

When we hit the place at a lope where the gopher colony had been uprooted, I forgot about the cow. One misstep and my horse and I would go down in a cloud of dust. Certainly one or the other of us would be lame after such a wreck.

Cricket was one of the more sure-footed horses I'd ever ridden. The only time he'd ever gone down on me was when he'd once lunged to turn a cow on the feed-ground, in straw on top of ice.

There wasn't anything I could do to contribute to his effort, so I just pitched him the reins and sat back - careful not to disturb his balance. The measured Ta-Da-DUM of his hoofbeats lost their cadence as he hop-scotched through the maze of holes. Cricket seemed only to let a hoof touch down where there was solid ground. I don't know what he did when there was a hole in line with his next foot-fall, but it felt like he skipped some steps and made up the difference with an extra two steps the next round.

We came out the other side of the badger patch, both of us still upright, and Cricket picked up the pursuit of the recalcitrant cow. In the meantime, Wendy had seen the attempted escape and had joined the chase. But just as we hit stride again, I had to pull up as the cow ducked around a soap-hole.

As I said, this field was around Alkali Lake - a stinky, dead body of water surrounded by chalky grey clay. The "soap-hole" was a place about 2 miles away where moisture had bubbled up through the gumbo soil in a manner similar to quicksand in another part of the country.

A remnant of barb-wire surrounded the truck-sized quagmire, and some fenceposts stuck up in warning. The cow saw this vestige as the only hint of cover on the open prairie and swerved behind it.

Wendy and her Arab were closing fast. Too fast. The horse was typically hot-blooded, and he was still green. He didn't understand why his rider would be trying now to steer <u>away</u> from the cow. Pulling up Cricket, I watched as Wendy and her horse dropped into the muck.

Out away from the treacherous and twisted wire, I tied Cricket's reins down to his leg to keep him from straying. As I reached the thrashing bodies in the soap-hole I realized the problem that had Wendy near tears: she wasn't concerned about herself, but about the Arab who had on a tiedown that kept him from getting his head up out of the slop!

Her attempts to release the snaps on the tie-down were in vain. But after a little coaching, Wendy grabbed the headstall and pulled it down over the little horse's ears. That freed his head and eased his struggling. I extended a hand and pulled Wendy up on solid ground.

There's no telling how deep that hole is. And the bank seemed to be undercut. Even with his head free the Arab couldn't find footing to get out of the goo.

After clearing a path through the rusted wire to the soap hole, I brought Cricket up. Wendy took the end of my lariat back into the mud to knot it around the horse's neck in a way that the loop wouldn't choke him.

But even though Cricket was half again bigger than the Arab, we couldn't pull him out on a straight pull. The horse's chest would hit the solid bank and hang there, stretching out his neck. Wendy reached down into the slop to release the cinch. But even with saddle off the horse wouldn't budge.

Maneuvering along the soap-hole, Cricket and I pulled Wendy's horse in parallel to the bank. Then we doubled around, pulling the Arab's head out, around, and back, rolling him up and over onto the dry ground.

The horse just lay there for a while in the dirt, looking pathetic. All four of us were drained. The cow had long since wandered off to join her compadres.

The pasty grey-brown mud was everywhere - all over the horse, the rope, the saddle, and the rider. There was no clean water to wash it off. My handkerchief had only enough capacity to wipe off Wendy's face. My comb just arranged the mud in her hair.

But we had cows to deliver. Slinging off the worst of the mud, we re-saddled Wendy's horse and resumed our mission.

The cows hadn't strayed too far, and the bunch-quitter had circled around to hide in the middle of the herd. We barely kept up with the cows as we headed them down the lane and into the corral.

Later, back at the house, Wendy wasted no time getting a shower and clean clothes. We hosed the worst of the goo off our gear. But ten years later there is still a trace of mud in the crevices of that saddle. And ten years later, I suspect that horse will still yield to the reins when his rider signals to pull him off a running cow.

The Lawyer

Early one winter, I got a call from a nearby lawyer for whom I had done some shoeing. He was planning a vacation and needed someone to look after the cattle in his absence. Things were pretty slow that time of year and I was on the lookout for anything that paid cash, so I told him that I could do the job. We arranged for me to stop by and look over his situation a few days before his departure.

On the appointed day, I headed out to see his ranch. It was a beautiful place, about 10 miles from the town where he practiced, and he was quite proud to be the new owner. It seems that he had traded his house in town as a down payment to the old folks who had been the previous occupants. Much of the land on the ranch was obviously enrolled in CRP - Conservation Reserve Program.

CRP had been initiated by the federal government a few years before to take millions of acres of farmland out of production. In order to buoy the price of grains and to reduce soil erosion, the Department of Agriculture had paid thousands of farmers to seed marginal farmlands back to grass. The contracts called for them to maintain the land in grass for 10 years with no grazing allowed. In return the government gave them an annual payment for keeping the land idle.

The program did help control erosion and improve groundwater, and it was a boon to western farmers. Many had elected to take the guaranteed annual income rather than continue to farm minimally productive land. With most of his new ranch in CRP, this man had found a way to acquire land with minimal investment while the taxpayers made his payments.

The lawyer had dreams of being a cowman, and had bought a horse and a few yearlings to stock the pastures that were not enrolled in the program. He had a Blue Heeler Dog and a pickup, a pair of expensive boots and a western cut suit.

He was dead serious as he led me around the place to show me what needed to be done in his absence. We measured the cat food and dog food just so. We selected some nice green hay for the horse and gave him his ration of grain. Then we headed out to feed his "herd". We were careful to close the gate behind us as we went into the field with the yearlings, then headed over to the little creek which wound its way through the pasture. I just watched and nodded my head as the lawyer took the axe and broke the ice along the bank for 50 yards so the cattle could drink.

The yearlings had spotted us by this time and had ambled over to see what we were doing. They knew the routine and followed us over to the stackyard where their hay was piled. I shooed them away from the gate as we drove through, and I closed it quickly behind us.

I moved to open the tailgate of the pickup so that we could throw the hay in, but the lawyer cautioned me to leave it up. He explained how he had learned a hard lesson the first time he loaded that pickup. When he had thrown on the first bale from the top of the stack, he said, it had lit hard and sprung the tailgate. After paying $130 for a new one, he knew better than to leave it open the next time.

The cattle gathered around the fence as we tossed the bales over the sides and into the bed of the pickup. The fence was loose, and several of the yearlings had their heads through, scratching their necks on the wire. It didn't take long to get the hay loaded - we need only eight bales - then we had to battle our way through the herd to get out the gate.

180

The lawyer drove the pickup out into the field and stopped. He showed me how to carry a bale out away from the pickup, cut it open, and spread the hay out in every direction. We got back in, drove ahead, and repeated the operation seven more times. As we drove away, his herd was munching contentedly on their fodder.

By the time we got back to the house, I was chomping at the bit. I was late for an appointment in town. I hadn't counted on two hours to feed 36 head! We hurriedly settled on a price of $15 a day for my service, and I made tracks down the road.

On the first day of the lawyer's vacation, I went out to feed his stock. Without him to tell me how, it took a lot less time. Feeding the pets took only a moment - they could have all the feed they wanted in this cold weather. I didn't waste time giving oats to a fat and idle horse. And I knew the cattle wouldn't bother the open gate as long as I was in the field with their hay.

The old rancher who had owned the place had more sense than the lawyer. He had strategically placed a couple of large rocks at a shallow place in the creek. The rocks produced a riffle which kept the water open in almost any weather.

I hurried to the haystack and threw on a load before the cattle had time to get in my way, and headed back out to feed. With the pickup in low gear, I stepped out, flipped up into the back, and flaked the hay slowly over the side, then headed back to the stack. The yearlings now had their minds on breakfast and didn't follow me -there was no reason now to close the gate as I put a good load on the pickup.

With the tailgate open, I laid in what bales were on the ground and then backed up tight to the stack. It was easy and safe to pull the top bales down onto the base of hay that was now in the bed of the pickup. While I was at the stack, I put on a moderate load of 36 bales from which I could feed for the next week.

After ten days of vacation, the lawyer and his family came home. But he had contracted with me for two weeks since he was leaving again for some convention. I saw his wife through the window as I drove into the yard to feed the next day.

With my chores organized and laid out, I had his two hour regimen cut down to twenty minutes. When I had finished, I dawdled around for awhile. Ranch wages at that time were pretty low and fifteen dollars would buy a lot more time than half an hour. I didn't want it to appear that I was ripping them off.

But there was simply nothing more to do. I got impatient with hiding out, and convinced myself to leave. I was not being paid for the time, I told myself, but rather for the job. And the job was done. My efficiency was worth fifteen dollars.

For a while I felt guilty about charging so much for so small a job. I hoped that the lawyer's wife wouldn't get angry over my being paid $30 dollars an hour for feeding cattle. But she later told a friend that she had been watching my technique and appreciated my efficiency. She had suggested to her lawyer husband that he might learn something from me.

My conscience was finally appeased when I rationalized that I was only being paid $5 an hour for the work - the other $25 an hour was for the education of a high-priced lawyer!

Jim's Mule

Most years in north-central Montana, we get a rainy period in early June. Along with the accumulated ground moisture from the winter's snow, this can make a fair hay crop some years. Most ranchers, however, don't depend on the benevolence of the weather for their livelihoods. Most have some means of irrigating their haylands.

The first cutting of Montana hay begins in late June. With irrigation, alfalfa shoots up again and is ready to be cut a second time the middle of August. On years when there is enough sun and enough water, there can be a third cutting of hay in the warmer areas.

This year had been different. Another wet spell had hit in August, holding up the second cutting. We are always glad for moisture on the east side of the Rockies, and no one was much bothered by it this time. But it was setting the haying back by several weeks, and a guy has to worry about frost when haying lags into September. Another problem with the late haying: Early Bull season opens for elk on September 15.

Montana is a state of hunters. Almost every male in the state has a few guns, and he likes to use them. Deer abound, and hunting is also good for upland birds, waterfowl, antelope, mountain lions, mountain Goats, Mountain Sheep, black bear, Grizzly Bear, and Elk. Montana is split in two by the Rocky Mountains, and in the middle of the northern Rockies is the huge expanse of the Bob Marshall Wilderness. It is a primitive area where no vehicles are allowed, and elk hunting is the number one pursuit.

In early September, hunters with their horses come from all over the world for pack trips into the "Bob". A large percentage of the trekkers are professional outfitters with their out of state clients. But also well represented are farmers, ranchers, and horsemen from around the state who are making their annual pilgrimage into the wilderness. Among the regulars to the mountains, was Jim Sheble, a farmer from Valier.

Jim had a nice place, and did a good job farming it. He was a responsible man who did each task efficiently, and in good time. But he was never too busy with the farming to make at least one trip into the mountains and over the divide to the Wilderness.

Jim had a couple of saddle horses and a pack-mule, and I had been shoeing them for him for several years. So, it was not at all unusual that I would find myself shoeing them again. But something did seem a little different this time.

As I worked, my mind felt a little foggy. The movements of leveling the feet and shaping the shoes had come to be automatic over the years, and I could easily carry on a conversation as I worked. Jim was standing nearby, watching and visiting as I nailed fresh iron on his mule.

But I felt like I was emerging from some kind of strange dream as I looked up and observed my surroundings. The grass was looking mature, and the sun was at an angle which showed that the summer was over. I knew where I was, but I couldn't be sure of the day or year.

Still trying to get my bearings, I said "I'm shoeing your mule, so it must be Fall and the haying's all done."

"It's Fall," replied Jim, "but the haying's not done. Are you all right?"

I pondered his words as I continued to work. Then I noticed the heavy cotton rope knotted around the mule's neck and looped behind her rear foot.

"This mule's foot is tied up and my cheek hurts," I said. "She must have kicked me."

"She did," Jim answered. "Maybe I should take you to the hospital."

Well, I was as tough as any mule. And just as stubborn. I refused his offer and finished the job. By the time I had all my gear put away, my mind felt clear again.

A mule is sure-footed and quick, and this was the second one to catch me. The first time had been while shoeing a Forest Service mule in Lincoln 10 years before. Both times I had been stooped over with a forefoot between my knees when the mule had come up with the hind foot on the same side and struck me in the head.

The next time I saw Jim, the day was still fuzzy in my mind. What I remembered seemed a little strange, so I quizzed him about the episode.

"Sure enough," he said. "I heard a 'thwack' that sounded like a pumpkin hitting the ground, and you staggered away with your arms out to the sides. I thought you must be hurt, but you just went over to your outfit and got some rope to tie up her leg."

I have always prided myself on being a reasonable man. But with a history like that, it sure is hard to refute anyone who says I have a thick skull.

Farmer Horse

Dave Turner was another farmer who loved his time in the mountains. It was summer, the field work was caught up, and he was itchin' to get off the dusty dry flats and into the cool, green, lush mountains. So Dave gave me a call and said he had four or five horses to shoe.

The day I headed up into his area I had a car-full. Along with a few of my kids, my dad came along on this trip. Dad was raised on a farm himself, and has plenty of his own tales about livestock. It was through his genes that I received my love for horses. But the Great Depression had shown him the value of an education, and he had chosen to spend his life as a professor.

Now, you understand, there hadn't been any pressure on me to be a teacher. Really! All the opportunities were provided, of course. But I wasn't pushed. And for twenty years, my folks supported me in my choice to be a cowboy.

Being a professor, Dad had the summer off, and the folks had stopped by to visit us for awhile in Montana. So today, Dad was in the Suburban with me and the kids, on the way to shoe horses north of Cut Bank.

I don't know where the conversation had been headed, but Dad had a thought he was compelled to mention. "You know," he said, "if you were a teacher, you could still have your summers off to shoe horses."

My kids just hooted! "Dad?! A teacher?! You've got to be kidding!" And that was the end of that subject.

We finally got to Dave's place, and I questioned him about the "four or five head." "Well," he said "I have five head, but I don't think you can shoe the fifth one." I just grinned at my kids.

Of course we could shoe him. I could shoe *anything* with hooves and hair.

The stock was typical 'farmer' horses: only half-broke, and the other half spoiled - the kind of horses that really make a shoer work. They couldn't decide whether to lean on me or pull away. But I'm a cowboy, and I advertise "mules, broncs, and colts a specialty."

Most times, a shoer's visit is a good time to catch up on doin's around the country, and I usually work with an audience. We swapped stories all around while I worked, and we had the first four horses done just in time for dinner.

I was moving a little slower when we went back out to finish up. I really hadn't needed that second piece of pie.

Dave was a little worried about that last horse. He told how his buddy had attempted the job last year. It had been quite a fight. They'd been upside-down and right-side-up and all tangled in rope. They'd finally gotten iron all around, but when the dust had cleared, the horse and the shoer were both too lame to go to the mountains!

This horse was a good one to ride, Dave said, and he'd really like to have shoes on him. But it wasn't worth getting someone hurt.

For me it wasn't a question of *if* I shoed the horse, it was a simply a matter of how much gear was involved. My outfit was well-supplied with ropes, hobbles, straps, halters, and nerve lines. The last man to try this horse was an <u>amateur</u> - rough horses were my business. I had enough sense to be careful, but not enough to quit.

I moved slowly as I began work on the grey's feet. He was snorty, he was goosey, and I didn't trust his teeth. He never relaxed a muscle. I had to keep talking, and move slow so as not to startle him. He made me work to pick up a foot, then he

188

leaned on me. I was holding up nearly half of his weight. Through the whole process, the grey was a tightly coiled spring. Any time I tried to shift his weight off of me, the horse would pull away and snap his foot back to the ground.

The grey _was_ dangerous. They say ignorance is bliss; if Dave hadn't been so ignorant, he would have been afraid to ride him. But I had three shoes on. I'd managed this horse with sheer finesse, and I was nearly done.

Things deteriorated pretty fast as I worked on the last foot. I was getting tired and the horse was getting impatient.

I eased my hand from his hip down the leg and picked up the foot to trim and level it. My knees struggled to hold up the weight which he transferred onto them. A few times there was a mutual decision between us to set his foot down quickly. But we were almost done!

The fuse on this horse was slow, but his powder was dry, and suddenly I was knocked to the ground by the force of his explosion. I hit the ground crawling to avoid his heels. There was an explosion of splintering wood and clanging metal as a hoof hit dead center on the box that held my shoeing tools.

I lay in the dirt amidst the nippers, nails, and pieces of wood that were blown in a thirty-foot radius in back of the horse. My Dad was quiet. Dave was white. I don't know who _he_ was more worried about - me or his horse.

I checked myself over to see if I was hurt, then began gathering the scattered tools into a bucket. I stifled the urge to imbed the claws of my nailing hammer into the grey's forehead, right between his eyes. The time for gentleness had passed.

I was determined to teach this horse to stand for shoeing, so I went to my trailer and pulled out a war bridle. With it I could put pressure on the horse's mouth whenever he pulled away.

Most horses quickly learn to avoid the pain by standing still. But not the grey. I jerked so hard on the line that it broke.

There is no question but that horses weren't domesticated until after rope was invented. My next step was a half-hobble on his pastern and a rope knotted in his tail. I started pulling up the slack, planning to pull the foot up into a handy position and let the tail hold the weight of the foot while I nailed on a shoe.

But rather than the foot coming up off the ground, his hip started to drop down. A slap on the butt got the horse upright again. That's when he began to kick.

He jerked his leg forward then kicked out back as he tried in vain to reach whatever it was that had a hold of his tail. When he slowed down, I tried again to pick up the foot to put in some nails. But the action of his hoof matched the look in his eye - he was out for blood.

Another trip to the trailer for a rope to cinch his leg up toward his neck and shorten the travel of his kick.

It's hard to say which one of us was working the hardest. Sweat was dripping off both the horse and me in about the same proportion. I was working against his 1300 pounds, and he was working against the ropes.

With his leg immobilized, at least he couldn't lay on me. But his foot was at an awkward angle, and I was working upside down. I could have thrown him all the way to the ground, but then I'd be working sideways. And I never figured a horse learned anything on his side.

When I reached under the horse to grab his now-immobile foot, he pulled it further away from me - and sat right down on the ground!

We slapped him with a rope. We kicked him in the ribs. We bounced on his chest. But the grey just lay there and glared at us.

Finally I grabbed his nostrils and pinched them shut. A horse is strictly a nose-breather and it didn't take him long to run out of air. With a violent heave he was back on his feet.

The horse was starting to weaken!

With my sweaty shoulder against his heaving ribs I leaned under and grabbed his foot. Laying the shoe on the bottom of the hoof, I stuck in a nail and gave it a whack. With every blow of the hammer the horse would jerk, but each successive pull was less violent.

It took five raps apiece on each of the eight nails, then twist off the excess. The grey's head was drooping. Another round with the hammer to tighten the clinches, and he hardly flinched. Pull the nail-ends down with the clincher, and dress off the hoof with the rasp, and I was done.

All the fight was gone from the horse as I untied the ropes. We gathered all the equipment and packed up the ropes. Dave handed me a beer along with the check. I had taught a horse a lesson, and the farmer would go to the mountains with all five horses this year.

Dad was still quiet as we drove away. It was a couple of miles down the road before he finally spoke. "You know," he said, "the next time someone tells you a horse can't be shod, maybe you shouldn't take it as a personal challenge!"

Anvil

I'd been shoeing horses that day in that huge flat country between the Two Medicine River and all of Canada. You can see for miles in every direction, with only the Sweet Grass Hills off to the northeast from which to get your bearings. We had stopped in Cut Bank to get gas on the way home, and that's when I noticed that the tailgate on my shoeing trailer was open. I immediately felt a sinking feeling in my stomach. When I hurriedly assessed the damage, I discovered that my anvil was gone!

It was October, and I was in the middle of my fall run of shoeing, leading up to hunting season. I had scheduled eight horses for nearly every day for the next two weeks, and an anvil was a necessity. I had a couple of my kids with me on the expedition, and all eyes were on the road and the borrow-ditch as we retraced our route.

This was a big old anvil that I had gotten 20 years earlier from a friend of my grandfather, who had retired from a metal fabrication business. Without it I could not fit horseshoes. My business – my whole life - was on hold.

Two hours later we had been the 30 miles up the road going back to the place I had last used the anvil, and down it again still looking. If it had landed in a place visible from the road, then it had soon been spotted and claimed as the treasure it was.

That evening I got on the phone to reschedule my shoeing. First thing next morning I called my shoeing supplier in a panic.

I'd been getting everything I needed – shoes, nails, rasps, and tools – from Mike Williams at Logan, Montana. A message on his answering machine was enough to be confident that whatever

I needed would be delivered in a couple of days. On this morning I spoke directly with Mike to discuss sizes and styles of anvils, and he assured me he would get one on the way.

There were plenty of tasks at home to keep me busy all day, but my mind was still on that anvil, and how I would catch up the lost time in my schedule.

It was late in the morning of the next day when the UPS man stopped at the house. I hurried out to see what he had brought.

An anvil! A shiny new anvil with a shipping label stuck right on its face. This was even a farrier's anvil rather than a blacksmith's anvil – lighter, and designed precisely for shaping horseshoes.

I was a day and a half behind, but I was back in business. I would get everyone's horse shod in time to meet their need. And more important - I would be able to make the house payment.

Appaloosa Filly

Doc Anderson had given me a call regarding breaking a filly for him. I rarely have passed up an opportunity for extra income, and am always happy to take on another horse to break. At $300 for 25 hours of labor, it sure beats working for a living.

A double advantage on this particular deal was that he wanted the horse broke to both ride <u>and</u> drive. That could mean a little extra time involved, which translates to a little extra money. I have always considered horsebreaking to be a family sport, and have usually involved at least one of my kids in the process. But when breaking to drive, there is room for a couple more kids on the wagon seat.

The only drawback to the project I could see was the breeding on the filly - half Tennessee Walker and half Appaloosa.

My Grandad had raised Walkers. The selection in their breeding has long been centered around their gait. This produced a strain of horses with a quick, easy, and smooth stride.

In breeding livestock, as with everything else in this world, there is a trade-off involved; you can never have it all. In the case of Tennessee Walker breeding, emphasis on the ability to pace has often been made at the expense of conformation. The strain of Walkers that Grandpa had bred tended toward deep, narrow chests with prominent backbones and disproportionately large heads.

The other half of the gene-pool of the doc's horse was Appaloosa, a breed which has been selected on the basis of color. Again, this emphasis has been done at the expense of some other traits. My experience with spotted-ass horses is that they tend to be endowed with IQ in inverse proportion to spots - the brighter the blanket the dumber the horse.

Everyone knows how "Native Americans" came to ride Appaloosas in the first place - it was the only thing the hunters could catch when they were afoot. Appaloosas are also the reason that Indians were such fierce warriors: you'd be pissed off too, if you had to ride an Appy all day.

Anyway, I took on the horse and began the process of breaking her.

As with all the rest of the animals in this world, including human animals, every one has a different personality. This filly turned out to be extremely quiet and gentle, and extremely stubborn.

We had her working pretty well under the saddle when we started her on the buggy. My breaking rig was a four-wheel rubber-tire outfit I'd picked up in a horse trade somewhere. Because the horse was so quiet, I had no trepidation in taking my kids along on my jaunts to acquaint the horse with all "dangers" lurking in the world - from shadows on the ground, to kids, dogs, and semi-trailer rigs.

This was one horse I didn't worry much about runaways. In fact, the biggest trouble I had was in getting her to start the buggy. Nearly every day I had to begin our drive by going to her head and leading her into pulling the load. She just didn't want to lean into the breast collar.

We worked the horse until she seemed safe for the good doctor to handle, then called him to pick her up. Before he loaded her into his trailer I threw one of the kids on her back to demonstrate the satisfaction of our standard guarantee - the horse did indeed neck-rein in a halter, bareback.

I smiled all the way to the bank with the check. And promptly forgot about the horse.

It was two years later when I heard from Doc Anderson again. He was soon to be wed, and intended to use the horse in the ceremony. The wedding was to be in a fashion typical of trans-plants from the East - the affair would be conducted with a Western flavor and would conclude with the new couple riding together into the sunset in a buggy pulled by the appaloosa.

In the meantime, the filly had grown into a mare. She had been ridden very little, and driven not at all. Wisely, the Doc had contacted me well ahead of time to ask me to tune up the horse before the ceremony.

In addition to his house in town, the Doc also had a place about 50 miles out, in the Little Belt Mountains. It was here that the horses were kept. One evening I got the idea to make a family outing of a trip to the doc's "ranch". We would drive up there and take the horse for a spin, then go on up the road and have supper at the restaurant nearby.

At the ranch we quickly caught the horses. The filly had grown in both size and character in the two years since she was broke. We harnessed her to Doc's Amish buggy, then led her to the hayfield for a little refresher course.

My sons Ted and Ben, then aged 9 and 12, climbed up in the buggy to join me in the drive. I stepped in, picked up the reins, and clucked to the horse. No response.

I pulled her head a bit to the left as I flipped the opposite rein against her rump. The horse just stood there.

Pulling her head to the right, I tried again to start the mare. She didn't move.

Handing the reins to Ben, I stepped to the horse's head. I pushed, pulled, and moved her head from side to side. Finally the mare came untracked and started to move the buggy.

The buggy was light. It was a one-seat, spring-mounted sports job used by some Amish school teacher to go to town for groceries. The Appy really had no excuse not to work. But it had been two years since she had been asked to pull, and she seemed to take offense at the request. It took some time to get the horse to step into the breast collar and go.

As I practiced the horse on starting and stopping, she began to shake her head and paw the ground. She was working up a good mad at the indignity of being hitched to that buggy.

I was getting a little nervous about her attitude and told the boys they'd better get down. But they didn't want to be left out of the action, so they climbed over the seat and stood in the wagon-bed where they could bail out if necessary.

We were about halfway across the hayfield when I felt the Appy bolt. The buggy lurched, my hat flew off, and the race was on! Ben gave his brother a shove to get him out of danger, then took a death grip on the back of the seat.

The field was on a sidehill, and only about 25 acres. The far fence was too near, and the ground was going by too fast. The specter of a collision with the barbed wire loomed in my mind and sent a chill down my spine. The horse, the harness, the buggy - they would all be injured in the wreck. And I didn't envision myself walking away from the tangled wreckage unscathed.

I pulled on the left rein to bring the charging horse around toward the uphill side. But we had enough speed, and the hill had enough slope that the near wheel began to rise off the ground. Too small a circle would cause the buggy to tip.

Another concern was the state of the wheels. This was a well-worn buggy, purchased second hand from an Amish farmer in the East. The wooden wheels had worn with age, and had contracted in the dry climate. They could easily over-center their camber and disintegrate into a pile of kindling.

I modified my course to compensate for the pitch of the land and the condition of the buggy. My circle brought us around just short of the fence.

The mare began to tire of her little game and slowed to a stop near the middle of the field.

With the ride now over, I climbed down and took hold of the reins at the mare's head. Ben walked out to recover my hat, then rejoined me at the buggy. We both shared our excitement and fears while regaining our composure.

We were yet a quarter of a mile from the barn. The mare needed to end her lesson on a more positive note. And besides, I wasn't about to walk.

Ted had enough of this horse and set out for the car afoot. Ben, after being assured that the runaway was over, climbed back up behind the leather-upholstered seat.

It took a little work to get the mare started again, but finally we were underway. It was only a few yards however, before the horse bolted again.

This time we were headed for home with the uphill fence on our right. There was plenty of room, and gravity was on our side as I again circled the rig around to the left. Staying upright was not as big a concern on this sweep as were the gopher holes throughout the field. We frequently hit the little dirt-piles, and the spring-mounted buggy would give a lurch.

A badger had also been excavating in the field, looking for a tasty morsel among the gopher population. He had left a particularly large hole in his wake, and a matching pile of dirt.

I was able to guide the runaway in the right general direction, but I was having a little trouble with the fine tuning. Both wheels on the right side hit the trough and peak directly. The 1-2 combination tore loose Ben's death-grip on the seat. He flew into the air and came down astraddle the rear axle.

From over my shoulder I heard a small, plaintive voice saying "Please stop her, Dad. I want to stop now."

When I finally got the mare under control again, Ben climbed down from his perch between the wagon-box and the wheel. There was a hole in the armpit of his shirt where the buggy tire had torn through the cloth. The horse was pretty well winded, and my arms were a little tired. I decided we could now call it a day.

I was able to keep the horse to a walk as we eased through the gate and around the barn. I cautioned the boys that there was no need to distress their mother with the details of our little ride.

The next day, Doc brought the horse down from the mountains. I led her from the corral to a flat, open field and hitched her up to my breaking buggy. It was of a more appropriate design, with a lower center of gravity, and hydraulic brakes.

But the mare wouldn't pull it. She would back, and she would rear; but she wouldn't tighten the traces. I had a horseback friend dally up the mare's lead-rope and try to get her started, but the Appy just set back against the rope.

It grieved me to be beaten, even temporarily, by an ignorant animal. But we were getting nowhere real fast. I would have to go back to square one with this horse.

Back in the corral I attempted to drive the horse with no load at all. But she had made the association with the blinder-bridle and the driving reins, and refused to budge. It took a fair amount of persuasion from a stock-whip to finally induce her to step out.

I was sweating worse than the horse when I finally turned her loose. I had been following behind her afoot, directing her with the long reins. It was far more work than I had anticipated, But at least I had her starting and stopping consistently again.

200

The next day I had her pulling a car tire around and around the arena. The dust that the drag threw up mixed with my perspiration, and caused a further deterioration in my attitude toward the mare.

On the third day I rigged the tire on the end of a chain. After she was pulling the tire well, I maneuvered her around so that the chain would catch under a small tractor tire and add to the weight she was pulling.

The Appy was already moving when she hit the heavier weight, and would not be pulling it from a standstill. Since the chain was not affixed to the bigger tire, it would slide off after a few steps, before she got discouraged with the harder pull.

The mare soon got used to the drill. She was starting the small tire well, and leaning into the pull of the additional weight when we snagged the bigger tire. The combined drag of the two tires was considerably more than the pull of the buggy.

A couple of days later, after the mare was accustomed to picking up, then losing, the extra weight, it was time to progress. I fastened the two tires together with a length of chain between them. Now the horse would start off the pull with the light tire, then pick up more weight after she was moving.

But the mare soon caught on to the idea that the extra weight was not dropping away as before. When she realized that I had her harnessed to a steady pull, she rebelled.

I wheedled and I coaxed. I hollered and cussed. I whipped and I beat. But all to no avail. That Appy mare refused to be made into a work-horse.

The doc was disappointed when I explained to him that this just wasn't the horse to use in his upcoming wedding. Had the mare been mine, I'd have found a proper home for her - in a pack string, maybe, or a glue factory.

I've broke all manner of horses for all manner of uses. Some of them were surely better than others. Even the Diamond D black had made a saddle horse before he returned to his habit of bucking.

But this time I'd been beaten. I had given it my best shot and failed. Maybe it **was** time to get a <u>real</u> job.

Parade

We were in the peak of calving at the Gordon Ranch south of Cascade, when the weather turned bitter. It had felt like spring when we first brought the cows in from the winter feedgrounds to the ranch headquarters, and we'd spent a pleasant afternoon ahorseback cutting out the heavies and pushing them into the calving field.

Steve Gordon had a good system: He put the heavies on a hillside just above the calving shed where they were spread out over a field that was small enough to look through quickly, yet large to give the cows clean ground and room enough to avoid the stress of confinement. When the new calves had their legs under them – four or five days after birth – he pushed them across the creek to a larger open hillside for another week or two until they were traveling well enough to move over the ridge and down into Richardson Creek.

But in the middle of calving a big storm dropped the temperature and dumped a couple of feet of snow. Traveling across the snow was too difficult for new calves, so the cows had all been pushed into a lot next to the calving barn. The herd was far too big to keep the cows in the barn, so we monitored that lot 24 hours a day and quickly moved each cow into shelter as she calved.

The preferred strategy was to spot a cow that was in active labor and work her into the barn where she could calve in comfort in a well-bedded stall. Sometimes, however, a fellow got busy with something else and a cow would calve out on the hard-packed ice of the lot.

A calf can stand a tremendous amount of cold if he is dry, has a full belly, and has some insulation between him and the frozen ground. But a calf enters the world soaking wet, and even with an attentive mom he can quickly succumb to hypothermia when he is rudely pushed out of a nice warm womb and onto the snow. A good stockman tries to keep his cattle bedded in straw, but a cow often leaves the straw-pile to find a more isolated place to calve.

I was driving a tractor out to feed when I spotted a wet new calf lying on the snow in the calving lot, so I jumped on a horse that was tied to the fence, dallied the rope from the sled to the saddle horn, and rode out to bring him in. Of course I wanted his mother to come in with him, as a full belly is an essential part of the equation. I aimed to get the pair of them into a "jug" – a small pen in the barn – where the two could be isolated until they had adequately bonded and the calf was ready to face the weather outside.

When I reached the far end of the calving lot I found a second new calf, and figured to make a quick turn-around with the first one and return for number two. Dragging the first new calf into the sled, I waited until the cow had looked over the contraption and had a good sniff of her calf that was now lying inside it, then I started toward the barn with the sled in tow. As I had hoped, the cow followed her calf.

What surprised me was that the second calf – still wet, but already up on wobbly legs – began to follow the first cow, who was following her own calf in the sled. This wasn't completely unexpected behavior – it takes a calf a day or two to figure out exactly which of the large animals nearby is his mother. A new calf will even follow a horse that comes near.

This second calf had a good mother, and she followed her baby, mooing her alarm. So now I had **four** animals in a line behind me: the calf in the sled, his mother, a second new calf following her, and the mother to the second calf in the rear, bellowing her indignance that her calf was departing without her.

Then I saw another cow walking along the fence with her tail held crooked and high – it was obvious that she was in labor. It would certainly be beneficial for her to calve in the barn where it was relatively warm, and save the stress on the calf of being dumped out into that frigid world, and of then bringing her calf in separately. So I pulled my horse in behind her and brought her right up the fence toward the barn. Now there were *five* cattle in the procession – one in front and four behind - plus me and my horse!

With the entire gather pushed, pulled, and lured into the barn, I sorted the two pairs and the calving cow into three separate jugs, shut the gates, tied up my horse, and stepped into the warm-room to pour myself a cup of coffee and gloat about my fruitful sweep through the cattle.

Four Wheelin'

When I hired on to the Gordon Ranch for calving, Paul had been working full-time there for more than a year. Steve Gordon, the owner, told me a little of the guy's background.

Paul had been a computer programmer, Steve said, at a hospital in New York. One night, on the way home from work, he had been mugged.

The beating Paul took was severe. He had been unconscious for days afterward in the hospital. When Paul finally healed up he decided that New York was no place for a sane person to live. He and a buddy loaded up and headed for as far away from the city as they could get. The two young men ended up here on the Gordon Ranch, and that is a long way from New York. Paul was still working there a year later, and he seldom left the ranch.

One reason Paul rarely went to town is that he was a poor driver. In fact, he'd never learned to drive before coming to Montana. Life in New York City does not require a person to own a vehicle - public transportation is cheaper, easier, and faster. Besides, there's no place to park. The few times Paul had been to town since he went to work for Gordon's, he had to borrow an outfit from Steve. And it seemed like every time he did that, something went wrong. So Paul figured he was better off to just stay home.

When calving started, Paul was assigned the job of night man. He had a warm room down in the calving shed where he could rest between checks on the cows out in the fields adjoining the shed. Night herding isn't too tough a job. There's lots of time to read or take a nap while waiting for the next cow to calve.

When a rancher has enough help to designate a night man, that man can sleep all day.

During the first week of calving, things were pretty quiet. The weather was excellent and the cattle were out on the hillside of the south calving pasture. There were only about thirty calves born all week. We didn't need to bring in the cows at night, so Paul made his checks from the seat of a pickup.

One morning, Steve and I discovered that the bumper was torn loose from the pickup Paul had been using at night. Later that day, after Paul had caught up on his sleep, Steve asked about the bumper. With a red face, Paul explained that he had run over a big rock in the dark as he had been trying to look out the window at a new calf.

By the end of the first week, the pace of calving was picking up. And that's when we got hit with the first big snowstorm.

Steve, Paul, and I quickly settled into a routine for handling the calving chores. Steve took care of the calving during the days, Paul at night, and I did the feeding.

One morning, Steve and I looked out to see a pickup sitting in the middle of a snow drift inside a stack-yard. Paul had apparently gone out the night before to get a load of small square hay-bales for the manger in the lot with the heifers, and he had gotten the pickup stuck.

Most of the hay on the ranch was put up in big round bales. I fed them out with a large four-wheel-drive tractor pulling a processor that unrolled the bales onto the ground. When I fired up the big tractor, Steve threw in a tow-rope, and we headed over to pull the outfit out of the drift.

When we arrived at the stack-yard, the story of Paul's nighttime adventure was written in the snow. There was the green imprint where bales had tumbled off the pickup and into the snow when the pickup had lurched and bucked through the drift. A scoop was sticking out of the berm of snow shoveled out from around the wheels. You could read the disgust in the footprints that led across the field and back to the barn.

At first glance the pickup didn't seem too stuck. The drift was only about 18 inches deep, and not too far across. Paul had already dug out enough snow to allow the pickup to rock back and forth a few times, gaining momentum to plow through the drift.

Steve and I figured that the engine must have died and Paul had been unable to re-start it; otherwise, Paul could have driven it out. There had been some kind of intermittent electrical problem that we had not yet diagnosed, and the pickup had been having starting troubles.

On closer inspection, we found that there were tire chains on all four wheels. We sympathized with Paul's struggle in the dark to chain up the rig in a snowdrift with numb fingers and snow blowing down his neck.

Then we realized that the tires were dug down into troughs in the frozen earth - Paul had been grinding away for quite awhile.

The first project would be to start the engine. Power steering would be a benefit in getting the pickup free, as would power to the pickup's wheels. Merely as a diagnostic procedure, Steve turned the key. We were both surprised when the engine roared to life!

Next, we assessed how stuck the pickup really was. Steve put the pickup in gear, and slowly let out the clutch.

Again we were surprised - the wheels didn't turn!

I climbed down beside the stranded rig to look at the drive shafts. Both the front and rear shaft were turning, but not the wheels!

Now we knew exactly why the pickup still sat there: In the dark, Paul had gunned the engine and dug and clawed to get the pickup through the drift. It wouldn't go forward and it wouldn't go backward, but Paul had kept the pedal to the metal until both the front and rear axles had ceased to turn.

Steve and I looked at each other and shook our heads. Both of us had been in worse situations on plenty of occasions, but neither of us had ever done this kind of damage. Any time an outfit stops moving, it is time to get out and try something different.

Hooking the pickup to the tractor, we tried to pull it out of the drift. The tractor strained and the tow-rope stretched, but the pickup didn't budge. The wheels were frozen down into dirt, and the snow had hardened around it. We feared that something else would give before the pickup pulled free; the rig would have to wait until we got the Cat down there to do some plowing.

The outfit sat there in the stack-yard for two weeks before we dislodged it and towed it up to the shop. It was a few more weeks before we got time to tear into it and see where the trouble lay.

The damage was not as bad as we expected. One of the locking hubs on the front axle had sheared all the screws, and the splines had been worn off the pinion yoke on the rear differential. We robbed the parts we needed off another pickup out in the "bone-yard", and had the outfit going again before dark.

Paul can't really be blamed for what happened. Those of us who were raised in agriculture were driving before our legs were long enough to reach the pedals. Years of experience on a ranch teach a man what a rig will go through, usually, and when to go around. You learn to read how deep a drift is and how hard, and how far you can get before you power out. A guy can feel how much traction he needs, and how much he has, and when he should give up and hike.

Taking city-bred kid and stick him out in the dark by himself in the middle of Montana is just asking for trouble. But then, Paul hadn't learned much from that lesson.

None of this is to imply that an experienced hand never gets stuck. I'd had to call on the radio for help just a few weeks before when I got stuck in a four wheel drive tractor.

I'd been out to feed the yearlings and found myself on a side-hill where a thin layer on the surface of the field had melted under the bright mid-day sun. I was only a few yards above a drop-off into the creek when the tractor started to slide sideways.

It took only a few attempts at forward, then back, to determine that I was in a real pickle. Every movement sucked the hay-feeder and the tractor closer to the edge. The field leveled off a few feet from the creek bank, and the wheels might have caught there and held, but I wasn't going to chance that with $75,000 worth of equipment.

Steve answered my radioed distress call and responded with another four wheel drive tractor and a big tow rope. With all four tires on both tractors angled up the slope, we slithered and slid sideways across the field, the processor swinging mere feet from the edge.

It wasn't long after Paul buried the pickup that Steve had to call for help. He had taken a tractor down in a coulee to feed some cattle out of the wind. His tractor had slid sideways on the snow, and into a fence. It was my turn to pull him out.

We had a few nice warm days that melted most of the snow. I was moving some cattle ahorseback when I heard Steve give a shout on the radio. He needed Paul to join him over at West Hound Creek to help get in some yearlings. Paul headed down the road in the flatbed pickup as I pushed my bunch of cattle over the hill.

An hour or so later the pair returned, pulling the flatbed behind the tractor.

When I got back to the barn the pickup was in the shop. The engine ran fine, but the wheels wouldn't go 'round. Paul had gotten stuck in a snowdrift, and again he had torn the rig up trying to get out.

The damage was a little easier to spot on this one, but a lot harder to fix. The rear drive shaft was twisted in two, and a knuckle was broken on the front axle.

Paul felt really bad about the damage he had done. He was eager to make up for all the trouble. But sometimes it seemed that it was his eagerness that *caused* the trouble.

During the summer, Paul had another wreck. Running along a side-hill with the four-wheeler, he must have caught a rock hidden in the grass.

When I next saw him, Paul stood by the machine with his head hanging in embarrassment. There were no outward signs of damage to Paul, but the four-wheeler was hashed - the handlebars drooped and the fenders were buckled.

I have to defend Paul. He was an earnest and industrious fellow. Paul would have made a good Boy Scout: Trustworthy, Loyal, Helpful, Friendly, Courteous, Kind, Obedient, Cheerful, Thrifty, Brave, Clean, and Reverent. But he was dangerous on four wheels.

Flight Number 932

The winter of 1995 was another in a series of mild ones in Montana. Spring was a little rough. The weather was beautiful through the first week of February, and went to hell just as the cows began to get serious about calving. But let's back the calendar up by nine months to give you some background for the story.

The typical Montana cattle ranch is termed a cow/calf operation: a herd of cows is kept year 'round to produce calves for sale in the fall. The cycle starts in late May when the cows, calves, and bulls all are turned out to pasture. The sky is blue, the grass is green, the cows are willing, and the bulls barely have time to eat.

While the cattle in the pasture eat drink and make merry, the rancher spends his time putting up hay for the long Montana winter. The growing season is short in the northern latitudes, but the days are long. More grass is produced during the short summer than the cattle can consume, so a portion of it is cut and baled to be saved for the time when the weather is cold and the residual grasses may be covered by snow.

Haying is certainly not the favorite time of year for a cowboy, but when the haying is done, it's time to get ahorseback to bring in the bulls.

In August, after having served their purpose for the year, the bulls are gathered from out of the cow herd and returned to their monastic existence in a separate pasture. Meanwhile, during the fall and winter, the fruit of the bull's labor of love begins to ripen. Nine months later, beginning in February, the cows start dropping a fresh crop of calves.

There are a number of risks inherent in calving. Leading them all is the danger of the fickle weather: a calf is born wet and helpless, and he has very little reserve to cope with cold. Until his coat is dried off and his belly is full, the calf is extremely vulnerable. During a storm the cows must be watched constantly, and every calf must be brought in to shelter, for a few hours at least. And cows sometimes need assistance with deliveries.

So calving is a time of constant vigilance among the cattle. The cows must be brought in close to headquarters where shelter and facilities are available.

On larger operations there are too many cattle to keep penned up. Many ranches only bring up the cows that show to be near term, leaving the bigger bunch further from the barns. As these calve, the new pairs are pushed into outlying fields to make room to bring in more cows to calve.

The spring of '96 I was on the Gordon ranch, southwest of Cascade, in Central Montana. With 500 cows to calve, we had to keep the cows moving in from the "outside" bunch, through the shed, and out the other side with their new calves as soon as the calves were able to travel.

Steve Gordon had an excellent set-up. The south calving pasture was about 50 acres immediately adjoining the complex of sheds, lots, and corrals which made up the calving facilities. The cattle could spread out and eat hay on the hillside during the day, where they could be easily monitored, and be brought into the lighted lot at night.

Within a few days after birth, a calf is strong enough to follow his mother for quite a distance. On an open slope just to the north of the barn was a field where the new pairs were turned out. Just over the hill was the Richardson Creek field. We made regular passes through the pairs in this north calving field to strain out the older and stronger pairs and push them over the hill into Richardson Creek to join the "outside" pairs.

The system worked well. Richardson Creek was the perfect place for the young pairs that were a week or two old. There was plenty of shelter in the copious brush along the creek, last summer's grass was still plentiful on the hillsides, and the stackyards were full of hay. It was close enough to be readily accessible, and big enough that it wouldn't become crowded.

Steve had some good horses, and we used them regularly to sort off heavies, bring in cows to calve, bring in pairs that had some problem, and cut pairs out over into Richardson Creek. Of course it was a 7 days a week job, but it was a nice ranch and a pleasant job. Then came the stormy weather.

The temperature dropped, the wind raised, and the snow fell. We soon had over a foot of snow. It takes around thirty pounds of hay per day to provide for the maintenance needs of a cow. When the weather turns bad, it takes a lot more feed to keep her warm. In the severe cold a cow may consume an additional 20 pounds a day, and the job is continually impeded by wind, snow, and cold.

Snowstorms during calving are an "all hands on deck" affair. There is seldom enough help to do everything that needs to be done. Steve's shift with the cows during the day and Paul's shift at night overlapped by hours at both ends. I was in the tractor feeding from daylight until well after dark, for days on end.

When there is more work than can be done, priorities must be set. Our priorities were with the newest calves - there simply wasn't the manpower to do anything more for the pairs in Richardson Creek than to assure that they were fed.

After the storm blew itself out and the work returned to a more normal pace, I finally got back over into Richardson Creek ahorseback. While most of the cattle had weathered the storm in good shape, three calves had succumbed. The loss of those calves was disappointing, but not unusual – just one of the hazards of the business.

Later in the spring, as the weather improved and the snow melted, I spent more time ahorseback, checking cows, cutting out pairs, and doctoring calves. One day, Steve mentioned that I should get the three cows that had lost their calves out of the Richardson Creek field.

Each class of cattle - cows, yearlings, bulls, et cetera - has different management considerations. When possible, it is best to keep each group separate. Steve wanted these dry cows all together in a field down the creek and across the county road.

My daughter Wendy was visiting at the time. She had spent a dozen years of her childhood ahorseback beside me, but seven years had elapsed since we had the opportunity to work cattle together. We took on the assignment eagerly.

Steve had some excellent horses. Wendy and I each picked a mount that suited our individual styles and preferences, and jogged over the hill into the pairs.

One particular black cow - among several hundred nearly identical black cows - can be hard to pick out. Searching through the bunch, we had three possible identifiers for the cows we were after: numbered ear-tags, dried-up udders, and the behavioral difference from the cows with calves.

We timed the excursion so that we would arrive while Steve was feeding. This would draw the cattle out of the brush and into lines along the windrows of hay where we could make an orderly search.

Inside the field with the cows, Wendy and I rode along, one of us on each side of the column of merrily munching mamas. We checked the numbers on ear-tags and we looked for udders that were no longer full of milk.

Some of the cows looked up at our approach, and spoke softly to their calves. Others threw their heads in the air and set off looking for their babies. But one cow up the line caught my attention with her nervous movements.

This cow would dart into the cattle clustered around the hay and grab a few mouthfuls. Then she would quickly glance at us, and move away up the file of cattle strung out on feed. She wasn't looking for a calf - she was simply looking for escape.

Moving closer, I looked the cow over. Her bag had dried up, and her ear-tag - number 932 - was on my list. We moved in to cut the cow away from the herd. But rather than step out willingly toward the gate, the cow dropped her head and made straight for the brush. Wendy and I glanced at each other and grinned.

The horses needed no urging to break into a lope to turn the cow, but she refused to yield to our presence. The second time the cow veered past my horse, I pulled down my lariat.

Up and down the creek we ran, Wendy on one side of the creek and me on the other. The cow dodged in and out of the willows, plowing through the brush in places where a horse and rider couldn't go.

Finally the cow broke cover and headed back toward the herd. My aim with the rope was true; I pulled my slack and dallied. Pulling the cow to a halt, we paused for a rest. The cow panted and slobbered, and strained against the rope.

When we were ready to move again, Wendy circled her horse around to aim the cow toward the gate. I gave a little slack, and shifted my horse between the cow and the brush.

But we had not yet earned this old girl's respect. The cow ducked between our horses and headed back for the willows.

I dallied again and pulled her up short, but we had lost a little ground.

Again Wendy and I positioned ourselves to drive the cow toward the gate; again I gave the cow a little slack; and again she pushed past us. Before I could stop her we had lost more ground.

My mind was busy as we all stood in a bunch, mad and puffing. My horse was tired and my cinch was loose. This cow outweighed us by a couple of hundred pounds, and she was determined.

This time the cow didn't wait for slack. She simply began walking toward the brush, dragging me and my horse with her. I turned my mount away from the cow began to squeeze him in earnest, but we were helpless as the cow dragged us backward in the mud.

When the cow reached the shelter of the creek, she stopped to sulk under the first willow. I was losing patience. This cow needed to learn some respect, and it was up to me to teach her!

With a mad cow on the end of the rope, I was stuck. If I dropped my dally she would surely depart, taking an expensive lariat with her. Besides, a cowboy's honor does not allow a cow to win.

"Wendy," I said, "get off your horse, find a stout club, and chase that cow out of there."

"No way!" she replied. "I've done that for you once before."

"I can't do it myself;" I pleaded, "She'll get away. She can't hurt you - I have her by the rope."

Wendy could see my point. Being a dutiful daughter, she did as I asked. Careful not to get her boots wet, Wendy moved in with a stick and gave the cow a poke from behind the tree.

"Hit her", I hollered. "Really get after her." But the cow didn't budge.

By this time, Steve had the feeding done. He drove the tractor over to where I was sitting on my horse. Steve looked the situation over as he climbed out of the cab.

"Now what are you going to do?" he asked.

"You go in there and run that cow out," I said. "Wendy is just *aggravating* her. I wish I had my old dog, Kate - she'd make that bitch beller!"

Steve studied the situation a while longer. He pointed out that the mud was pretty deep over in the brush by that cow, and that he had no over boots.

I was ready to inflict some real harm on that cow. Holding onto my dally, I swung down from my saddle and let Steve crawl aboard my horse where his boots would be safe and dry. I tightened the cinches, then set off in search of a club.

Returning with a suitable weapon, I commenced to beating on the business end of that cow.

She bawled; she bellowed; and she blew snot. Her eyes blazed in anger as she strained at the rope trying to get at me. But she refused to leave the brush.

When her nose began to bleed, Steve called a halt. We were making no progress; it was time to give up.

With that decision made, we now had to figure out how to get the rope off. Had I been planning to rope a cow, I'd have carried a spare lariat. But I had only the one rope, and Wendy's saddle was not designed for roping. My attempts to educate the cow had only served to make her more stubborn and angry. Thus far, Steve had kept the rope tight and not allowed her to get at me. But now I needed enough slack in the rope to pull the loop off over her head.

Every time Steve threw her enough slack to loosen the rope, the cow would again try to take me. My movements were impaired by chaps, overboots, mud, and brush, and the cow kept me jumping for cover. Steve and Wendy, of course, thought my feinting and dodging was hilarious – in fact, I think Steve gave her a little extra slack just to watch the show.

After tiring of their game, however, I retrieved the piggin' string from my saddle bags and tied the cow's hind legs together. Grabbing her tail, I pulled the cow off balance and brought her to the ground. Steve gave me enough slack to slide the loop off her head.

When the cow quit struggling, I pulled the slip-knot on the piggin' string, then ducked behind a willow. Wendy moved in ahorseback and decoyed the angry cow while I made my get-away.

We gave the 932 a few days to cool off before we tried again, but she was easy to spot as we returned for her. Wendy and I were a quarter of a mile away when she jerked up her head, turned tail, and headed for the brush.

I thought she might move easier if we could pick up a few other cows with her, so we gathered some pairs and swept them toward her. But suspicious dry cows don't move at the same pace as concerned mothers with their babies. We didn't gain much ground before they all scattered.

We gave the cow plenty of room and didn't push her too hard, but she knew we were after her. I left Wendy to worry the cow down the creek while I rode ahead to open the gate.

On this trip the cow didn't defy our horses and barge past us – she knew now that we had strong medicine and were not to be trifled with. She was on the move and headed away. My theory is that a rope tight around a cow's neck keeps the blood in her brain long enough to improve her thinking. The next time she sees a man on a horse she gives to the pressure and moves away rather than trying to dodge past.

Slowly but surely we worked the cow toward the opening. We would grab a cow/calf pair and throw them her way, letting them all travel together as long as they would. But the dry cow was concerned only with her own safety, and the pairs would quickly fall out.

I was on the other side of the brush when the cow hit the fence line that ran perpendicular. I heard limbs cracking, and Wendy said "Here she comes."

The open gate was on my side of the creek. When the cow came across, I stepped my horse forward to turn her out. My presence startled the cow a little too soon. She wheeled to the right and crashed away down the creek, breaking off the gate-post as she went.

We had her out of the field, and moving like a fast freight. I told Wendy to stay with her while I stood the fence up so we didn't lose any of the pairs. By the time I fixed the gate and caught up with them, Wendy and the cow were another quarter of a mile down the creek.

Wendy and I talked to each other back and forth across the creek as 932 moved along through the willows between us. Wendy finally had a chance to explain that she'd lost a stirrup soon after we picked up the cow. She'd been cowboying (cowgirling?) for a half an hour, about half bareback.

I expected the cow to "brush up" and sulk at any moment. I knew better than to crowd her.

Maybe it was the cool weather, or maybe it was the lesson we'd given her a few days before, but the cow just kept plowing on.

Luckily, the gate at the bottom of the field was open - the cow never slowed down. But there was another gate just across the county road, and it *was* closed. The cow went through <u>it</u> without stopping, too.

Wendy followed the cow on down the creek while I patched the fence a second time. She really didn't know where we were taking the cow, and by the time I caught up, it was time to turn the cow south.

So far we'd never left Richardson Creek. The cow had been in the protection of the brush for all but the quick trip across the county road. Now it was time to break cover and head across the field.

It took less effort than I expected to force the cow out into the open. She had up a head of steam! The old girl took off with her head and tail in the air, straight south to Squirrel creek.

The cow surprised me again when she reached the creek, found a crossing, and kept on moving. It was only a quarter of a mile more to the field where a few more dry cows were already residing.

Leaving Wendy behind the cow, I circled wide around at a long trot to open the next gate in plenty of time.

When the cow came to the fence, we gave her plenty of room. She stopped and looked it over, deciding whether to go over, under, around, or through, while we hung back, holding our breaths.

Finally, the cow chose to move on up the fence-line. It wasn't far to the open gate.

As I closed the gate behind the cow, Wendy and I began to laugh. We had covered that mile between the fields in record time, Wendy riding the whole way off-balance without her second stirrup.

It was then that I noticed that my slicker was gone from behind the saddle. With our mission accomplished, we back-tracked our route searching for our lost gear.

The yellow slicker was easy to find, lying near the brush where we'd crossed the last creek. Now we had to find the missing stirrup.

We rode back into the Richardson Creek field, and over to the spot where Wendy had last felt the stirrup. She'd been in the middle of a storm, cutting that cow, when she lost the stirrup.

Wendy had assumed when it happened that her foot had merely slipped out. She didn't have time just then to worry about it. When she finally looked down, she discovered that the stirrup was gone, buckle and all.

We rode up and down the creek and out through the hayfield, but never found the missing stirrup. Some day it will turn up, bleached, dried out, and twisted - a memorial to the flight of number 932.

Doctor's Horse

I'd found my way into the healthcare business rather by mistake, and it had became a full-time occupation. Working in healthcare had led me away from the ranch country where I had worked for the last 30 years and I was eager to reconnect. When I heard of a good western branding to be held locally, where the calves were still being roped and drug to the fire, I had to be involved.

Although I still did some cattle work, horse-training, and shoeing on the side, I hadn't owned any horses of my own for a period of about 10 years. I knew that Doc Kegle had a horse and trailer that didn't get used much, so I asked if I could borrow them.

"That horse won't do you much good," he said. "He's never roped anything."

"That's fine," I said "I'll get by".

"And I don't want you to use spurs on him," insisted the doctor

"Well, I don't often use spurs anyway. "Oh, and can I get away with your trailer too?" I asked.

"You're welcome to the trailer, but it won't do you any good either. The horse won't go in it."

The doctor owned a small 2-horse trailer that had just enough room on each side of the divider for one horse to slide in. It <u>was</u> small and dark, but I had loaded uncooperative horses before.

On the day of the branding I threw my bridle, saddle, lariat, halter, and extra ropes into my suburban and headed out to where the doctor kept his horse and trailer. It didn't take long to catch the horse and connect to the trailer.

As the doctor had warned, the horse balked at the trailer door and refused to go in. But I quickly tied a long soft rope to the end of the lead-rope, passed it through the front of the trailer, and brought the end around under the tail of the horse. With the rope pulling on his head and pushing on his butt, it didn't take long for the horse to jump right in. We were on our way.

It had been about 8 years since I had been to a branding, but it was all familiar to me: pickup, trailers, equipment, and people were all arriving. The cattle were soon gathered into a corral, and the cows were cut back out leaving only the calves. The fire was lit and the ropers rode in.

This was not big ranch country, and as I suspected, there were lots of "town" ropers and not too many competent wrestlers. I spotted one fellow in particular who was obviously an "O.C". – Ostensible Cowboy. (Ostensible: *presenting* or *appearing* to be true.)

This guy was wearing a big tall hat, bib-front shirt, high-waisted canvas pants, and a fancy pair of chaps. He had an expensive hand-tooled saddle that had seen little use. The guy had WannaBe written all over him.

The only thing is, the guy obviously knew how to wrestle calves.

It didn't take me long to partner up with him. Most of the ground crew was struggling to get their calves on the ground and hold them there. But Gary and I quickly became an efficient team that could easily flip a calf on his side and restrain him with little effort. In spite of his attire, the guy _was_ a hand.

As we worked I told him that I had given up cowboying when I finally realized that I would never be able to afford a saddle like his with cowboy wages.

226

"Cowboy wages didn't buy this saddle," he said. "I'm a truck driver."

As at any branding, I watched for my chance to start roping. We had started out with five guys swinging lariats, and the calves were coming in fast enough to keep the wrestlers busy. But when things slowed down I pulled up my cinch, shook out a loop, and rode into the corral.

As the doctor had said, this horse had never been roped off of. He was afraid of the branding fire and all the people, and he was afraid of the calves. It took some effort to get in to make a throw.

When I dallied the first calf to the horn, the horse couldn't decide which to fear most: the calf wiggling behind him or the roar of the branding pot and crowd of people in front of him. It took some real urging to get the calf drug past the fire and into the hands of the wrestlers.

As the afternoon wore on the horse became more accustomed to the commotion and began to understand what was expected of him. He never completely overcame his timidity, however, and my legs were getting tired of "pedaling" him along.

The town ropers were dropping out, and the wind was coming up. Soon it was howling at 50 MPH, and there were only three of us left ahorseback. I got off long enough to trade my straw hat for a scotch cap.

The lariat I had brought along was a little wimpy for the job. It was really a heading rope rather than a heeling rope, and it was years old and had lost most of its body, making it harder to set up the "trap" in front of the calf's hind legs. I hadn't heeled calves in some 8 years, and my desk job had left me as soft as my rope. I was getting tired. But no one else was stepping up to rope, and there were a lot of calves left to brand.

The dust was blowing in our faces, and the fun had "gone with the wind". Now there were only two of us roping, and I was missing too many shots. But there were still calves left to brand.

My face was black with dirt and I was dead tired when I drug the last calf to the fire. That beer sure tasted good, and the grub tasted extra fine. I ate until there was no more room for another bite.

But I don't remember even a thank you as I loaded my horse. I was an outsider. And even though I had contributed as much to the job as anyone there, I don't feel like my efforts were appreciated.

In spite of the lack of expressed appreciation, I was satisfied. I had taken a green-broke horse and accomplished quite a bit with him. I don't know who else would have roped those 50 calves had I not been there. And there was one fellow who *had* noticed: Boyd Iverson was 80 years old and a sure 'nuff cowboy – *he* could see that the two of us were cut from the same cloth.

Trick Rider

I was shoeing some horses for Boyd Iverson out of Townsend and Ben had come along with me. Boyd had his 80th birthday that year, and was a little stiff in the joints, but he wasn't about to give up riding. His good saddle horse was short but stocky - appropriate for a man who wasn't too big himself, and who had *enough* trouble getting on a little horse.

Ten years had passed since we left the Blacktail Ranch up on the corner of the Blackfoot reservation. We had moved to town, and slowly weaned ourselves away from the livestock business and into health care. I was still doing a little horse-breaking and shoeing on the side, but Ben and I still missed the "good old days" when we lived on the ranch with a corral full of horses and plenty of riding to do.

While I was nailing shoes on Boyd's good cowhorse, Ben expressed his desire to get ahorseback. I knew Boyd to be a good cowboy, and a guy gets to know a horse while he is shoeing him. I judged this horse to be an excellent mount, so I told him this would be a good one to ride, as soon as I got finished with his feet.

When the last shoe was on, I handed the lead rope to Ben and grabbed the next horse. Ben inquired as to where he could find a bridle.

For years, we had been breaking horses for other folks. Our standard guarantee was that you could neckrein the horse bareback in a halter when we finished. Boyd's horse was well broke - there was no reason to dig around for anything more.

"A **cowboy** don't need no bridle," I told him.

So Ben flipped up on the horse's bare back, and trotted off down the lane.

Ben had been riding with me long before his legs were long enough to reach the stirrups. We had covered many miles searching for, and driving home cattle from the Blackfoot reservation. He'd ridden a variety of horses, and broke a few of his own. Just being astride a horse felt good to him for a while, but he was soon bored.

Loping across the hayfield and jumping ditches was a little more exciting, and it wasn't long until Ben noticed that the horse was clearing the ditches with more and more room to spare.

Then he noticed that the horse was jumping ditches that weren't there! It was about that time he lost his cap.

I was bent down shoeing another horse when I heard the sound of running hooves. As those hoofbeats came closer, I noticed that they weren't slowing down.

I thought to myself that Ben knew better than that - he'd been taught never to run a horse toward home.

With the sound getting very near, I looked up in time to see a very surprised expression on Ben's face as his horse dove under the lead-rope of the horse I was shoeing. The rope caught Ben under the chin and flipped him off backwards.

Ben did a complete back-flip, landing on his belly and sliding head-first.

He lay there for a while before he moved. At last, he turned to me and spit the grass out of his mouth.

"*A cowboy don't need no bridle*...." he said with a disgusted glare.

Horseshoer's Head

I had entered a new phase of my life: for the first time in years I now had "Real Job", working as the CEO of a small hospital in Montana. One of the services offered by my hospital was Physical Therapy, and one of the patients of that service was Kenny.

I first met Kenny as his mother pushed him down the hall in his wheelchair. He was completely helpless - his body bent and twisted – the result of a head injury suffered while shoeing a horse.

The story was that he had been kicked in the head while shoeing. Like any good cowboy he got up off the ground, finished the job, and turned the horse out. Back at the house Kenny had taken some aspirin to dull the pain, and had gone to bed. He didn't wake up in the morning.

The injury had caused an intracranial bleed, which resulted in massive brain damage. Most of his body was now useless, and it appeared that the lights were on but no one was home. Without the therapy sessions, Kenny's uncontrolled muscles would contract him into a tight little ball.

On one of his weekly visits to the hospital, I was visiting with Kenny's mother when Kenny awkwardly raised his right hand and began to rotate it.

"Roping?", she asked him.

"Uhh," Kenny replied. Then he began to trace letters on the tray of his wheelchair.

"B.. e.. - bear?" "Do you want me to tell him about roping the bear?"

"Uhh."

I had crossed paths with Kenny in the hospital a few times before, and had visited with his mother. But all I had really seen was his deformed body. I knew he had a Traumatic Brain Injury that had destroyed most of his motor control, and hadn't considered that his intellect would be intact. And now it was obvious that he was still able to use at least one hand – however haltingly.

"Kenny," I said, now speaking directly to him, "can you use a computer?"

"Uhh."

"Can you write out that story for me?"

"Uhh."

Some time passed before Kenny's mother one day handed me the print-out of stories that Kenny had slowly and laboriously typed out on his computer.

There were many spelling errors – some of them typical of cowboy who had no interest in academic achievement, and many which were the result of the poor coordination caused by his brain injury. What was obvious was his love for the cowboy life, which had been snatched away in an instant by the very animal that had been at the center of that life.

Also obvious was that Kenny was still alive inside that gnarled body. He must have been terribly frustrated and lonely – especially when people like me overlooked his existence, and instead talked over the top of him to his mother.

After I had read through his stories I ran into Kenny and his mother in a hospital hallway:

"You know Kenny," I said, now talking directly to him. "You and me's both horseshoers, and you and me's both been kicked in the head. But you're in that wheelchair, and I'm running this hospital. I guess that shows which one of us has the thicker skull."

"Uhh, uhh, uhh!" said Kenny with animation in his deformed body and sparkles in his eyes.

Grassy Mountain Cowboy

The following stories were written by Kenny Doig of Townsend Montana. He is a cousin to world-famous author Ivan Doig.

Kenny was struck down in his prime by a blow to the head from a horse he was shoeing, and was thereafter confined to crippled body that was hauled around in a wheelchair. He did have some use of his right hand, and he pecked out these accounts for me on his computer in 1997.

One morning Tim Tew and I were riding the forest permit on Spotted Dog creek. A big black bear crossed the trail in front of me, so I built to him. He was out-running me in the downfall timber, so I sicked Joker, my dog, on him. He ran him up a tree about fifteen feet above my head. We sat there looking at him trying to decide what to do. We finally decided to rope him.

Tim threw the first loop and he hit him in the back. Thinking back now, I think he was smarter than me and missed him on purpose because he was a better roper than me. I threw a loop and caught him around the neck, then he started up the tree. My dallies kept popping off the saddle horn, because of the angle. So I grabbed the rope, but he was big enough to start pulling me up. Tim grabbed on and we got him stopped. I put a half hitch on the horn and tried to pull him down.

The bear backed down the other side of a big limb and I could not get him any farther. All I could do was hang him or give him my rope. It was brand new rope so that was out. Every time I hung him and gave him slack he would claw at the loop. So I hung him about six times until he clawed it off. He was one mad bear. As we rode off he kept woofing at us.

* * * *

Tim Clark and I were riding one day, we were separated and I was going up a small stream, when I rode around a small brush and there a dead cow with a fair-sized bear feeding on it. When it saw me he took off, it was about a half mile to any cover. I finally outran him and got between him and the fence and stopped him. When he had stopped puffing hard and was rested a little he came at me for five or six jumps. Scooter, the horse I was riding, quit and ran off, the bear split and ran off in different direction. When I got control of Scooter again I rode in front of the bear and stopped him again. This went on for about a half hour until Tim showed up and I showed him the bear then I let him go.

* * * *

Tim Clark and I were riding another time and seen a sow bear with three cubs. We ran at them a yelling, she quit the cubs, and Tim started chasing two of them. I took after the runt of the three. I was riding Scooter again. Every time I would get close I would bail off him and try to catch it. But Scooter was no help. He would stop, and when I came to the end of reins I would do a back flip, I didn't dare turn loose of him because I didn't want to walk home. So I gave up and just herded the cub back towards ma.

* * * *

Roxy Kerns, Tom Davis, and I were pushing yearling steers back up country one day when I saw that they were going past the creek crossing. So I started down a ridge at a hard lope to turn them across. While I was going down the ridge we jumped a sagebrush. On other side of the bush we started to have some trouble.

There was a badger hole hid, when Hubert stepped in it he went in to a roll, Hubert was the best all-around horse I ever rode but not this day. When I was on top again after the first roll, I started to push off, when I was about half off, I remembered I was wearing overshoes in oxbow stirrups. So I had to pull myself back on again, for the next roll over. This time when I came up I had my feet out of the stirrups, so I pushed off again.

When it was all over Hubert got up and started to take off, so I got up to try and catch him. I took about two steps and decided there was something more important to do. So I got down on my knees and stuck two fingers in my mouth and started digging the mud out so I could breathe again. In little while Tom showed up with Hubert and we went back to work.

* * * *

I went to a team roping one Sunday at Jack Kelly's, I was riding Sacket, I had sold my good roping horse. This one was new at it and had a bad habit of running on the wrong side of the steer and making me head by roping under his neck.

This time I caught the steer but when we turned left he clipped the steer's hind feet with his front feet and we went down. I forgot to undo my dallies so when the steer hit the end of rope he pulled the horse into a roll over me. I had pushed off but I pushed off the wrong side. I lit on my back with my feet on top of the horse. So when he rolled over it was on me, he brought my feet up and put my knees in my ears. And once again I had to stop and dig the dirt out of my mouth to breathe - you would think I would learn to keep my big mouth shut.

The next day I had to roll out of bed onto the floor and crawl to the door and pull myself up to get to my feet.

* * * *

I bought a three year old colt from John McNeal, who was having trouble with him. He was typically Hancock breed horse. One of the times he blew up with John he had got John in front of the saddle horn then beat him with it. Whatever he would do he would go at it whole hog.

The first time I rode him in the corral at home and he tried me, but I survived, the next morning we went to

Jack Leibee's to trail cattle to summer pasture. When we went to start I let Dave Stenson get mounted first. When I got up the horse tied into me. I was doing good then Dave rode in to turn him back on the fence line, so I got ready for it. About half way through the turn Dave backed off and the colt changed directions fast and about left me standing in the air, but I survived it somehow.

On that first day he tried me hard three times, I learned one thing. You do not spur him with both spurs at the same time, you could use one at a time, but use two and he would buck every time. The next time I rode him, I learned another thing about him, he would be walking along and hop up in the front end and switch leads. He would keep doing this off and on all day until you would stay relaxed, and then he would start bucking.

He was an honest horse and did not buck on hill sides, in timber, or on holey ground. He was a very tough horse to break but he turned into a very good horse. He tried to do ever thing well weather it was getting you, or getting the job done. I named him Skip.

* * * *

Tim Tew, Dave Stenson, and I were riding sagebrush park country one day. Dave was riding a very green colt, all that the colt was doing was following our horses. We started down a hill into the timber on a trail. Tim looked back at me and nodded at me, I knew what he

241

was going to do. We started down the trail at a hard trot. The trail went under a tree that was leaning against another tree. There was enough room for a horse but not for a rider. We ducked around the trap, but Dave's horse didn't and left Dave hanging in the tree. We were laughing so hard his horse about got away.

* * * *

About two days before hunting season, we were getting the cows out of the Mannix Park area. Tim Tew, and Tom Davis were in a deep draw on east side of Mannix Park, they were making a lot of noise trying to get the cows out of there. I came up to the draw the other way and as I rode up there was a five point bull looking down into the draw at all the noise. I stopped about fifty feet behind him and got off. I was packing my 357 magnum pistol and took a bead on him. But instead I just hollered at him, it scared him so bad he almost fell down. I have always kicked myself for not shooting him I will never get a better chance to shoot a bull with a pistol.

* * * *

I was riding a little ways from Mannix Park, down through what was called the counting V. The counting V was a bunch of log laid out in a V to count sheep though. While I was riding through a bull bugled on the ridge. I whistled back at him with a plain whistling through my teeth, he was either one dumb bull or very horny bull. For

I whistled him up to about thirty feet of me, but he would never come around the trees to where I could make a run at him.

* * * *

Tom Davis and I were riding Deer Park area gathering bulls one day. We found two and roped them; we were trying to get them to the truck. They got the ropes crossed and we had to trade ropes, I tied the bull I had to a tree, and got off and was twisting the tail of Tom's bull. The bull ran up and hit Tom's horse, then ran off; he got away with my rope. We found him in the timber.

Tom got on one side to keep him distracted while I got down and tried crawling up to the rope and tie it to a tree. I didn't make it - he saw me and came after me. I had one wrap around the tree so I took off with the end of rope, but it looked like he was going to end up with more rope than me. So I cut and ran for another tree and ducked around it and about ran into him. For he ran on the other side already.

The next day we came back to get the rope off of him. We found him in a stand of lodge pole pine. We could not get close enough to rope him. So I went ahead of him, and put my loop between the fence and a tree so it was over the trail. Tom said wouldn't work, but it did. When I got him stopped, I took a wrap around a lodge pole and sucked him up to it then took a wrap around another pole. The bull went to fighting the capture and broke the tree off. When I got him sucked up to the other tree, Tom got a heel loop on him and we got him down so I cut head ropes off and then Tom turned him loose.

He was going up the trail along the fence line when he left us; we heard the fence being tore up when came to the corner.

* * * *

Don Shonka and I were riding back from pushing cattle back on the forest permit. We came back a different way than we rode up, we came out of the timber into a park. We rode into the middle of about twenty cow elk with calves. They ran in all different directions, we just kept on riding at a walk, when we looked back there was a calf elk following us. He was about ten feet behind us, he followed us about fifty feet until he came up and sniffed Don's horse then he cut and ran off.

* * * *

Mark Tisdale asked me to help him with his roping, so I watch him rope one cow. I decided the first thing was to break him of the bad habit of looking down as he dallies. So on the next cow I rode on the left side fairly close to him. When he roped the cow and looked down to dally I hit his hand hard with my doubled rope. He looked at me surprised I told him would he rather have a little pain or a lot when he lost a finger to the dallies. I only had to hit him one more time.

He was lucky he did not dally with his thumb down. That is really dangerous. If he had I would of had hit his hand real hard. The only other thing I could see wrong was that he was rolling his wrist at the wrong time to roll the loop over.

* * * *

I had a dog named Murphy who would jump where I patted if I said his name. Four of us were riding back to the barn one day, Dave was riding a green colt again. We were riding at a walk, Dave was on the left side of me. I leaned over and touched his colt on the neck and said "Murphy". When he hit the colt in the neck, the colt went to spinning to the left like a champion reining horse. Dave was a good rider and stayed with him, a lot of riders would have bit the dust.

* * * *

My first bear chase was when I still in high school. We were out getting lodge poles. Clay and Clint were cutting them down; Tim and I were a horse back dragging them out. We had just came in to the pile and looked up and saw a bear watching us. So we gave chase. When I was going at full speed I hit a limb that knocked me back behind the cantle. I rolled over backwards, my feet went up until the stirrups stopped them. Somehow I rolled

back up and got the horse stopped, I had to get off an
up-chuck to feed the flowers.

* * * *

We were gathering cattle out of the mountains and
someone pushed five head of elk out in the open - four
cows and a scrub four point bull. They were about one
hundred yards off when I gave chase. I was riding my
slowest horse. After about five hundred yards I was with
in thirty feet of them, but when I would get closer they
would start swerving. My horse could not keep up the
speed and change leads, we finally hit a down grade and
they left me in the dust.

* * * *

Dave Stenson and I were to the Mead Creek
pasture to doctor replacement heifers. Dave was doing
the heading - I was riding a three year old that was not
ready for heading. We came upon a two year old bull with
foot rot. He was on a hill side; I rode alongside the bull
to guide him up the hill while Dave headed him. Dave
missed, and I was right there so like an idiot I roped him.
I was not cinched up enough to be heading. Every time I
try to stop him, he would turn down hill and my saddle
would be pulled foreword. So I got real close to him, and
when we came to a tree I rode on the other side. I
slipped about thirty feet of rope before we came to a
stop facing each other. We traded ropes and then I
heeled him.

* * * *

We were feeding close to two thousand cows at
the Willow Creek ranch one winter. When we ran out of
hay, five of us trailed them to the Spring ranch which is
only about five miles. I wish I had taken a camera it was
some sight-seeing them strung over the hills.

* * * *

The first spring I worked at Rock Creek Ranch,
Lane Cook and I were riding up a draw during calving and
found a cow in trouble. I roped her around the neck then
I got off and hooked Lane's rope on. Every time Lane's
horse would pull, my horse walked foreword. As I walked
up to him to make him stay, Lane pulled and my horse
took one step and then started to pull back. That one
step put his left front foot on my left foot, when Lane
got done pulling and I got the horse off my foot, I knew
something was wrong. I couldn't stand on that foot.

Lane came helped me back on my horse. When we
got back to the camp I slide off and Lane took care of my
horse. I hopped around on one leg doing what little I
could do to help until it was time to go home. When we
got back to the ranch I hopped into the bunk house and
pried my boot off- which took a few tries to perform. My
little toe was broke so I moved it around until it looked
right then I taped it to the next toe.

For about a week I hopped on one leg, and Lane
saddled my horse. I couldn't ride with my foot in the

247

stirrup so I put a short rope around the saddle horn when I got on, then ran the rope around my leg and tied the other to the saddle horn too. This went on for about a week until I could put weight on my foot again. It wasn't a bad week - I didn't have to do any of the grunt work for a week.

* * * *

I was shoeing a ranch horse one afternoon. He had a tendency to lean on you. I got the left front foot done and had the shoe tacked on the left hind foot when he picked his right foot while I was holding his left one, I kept his leg up hoping he would put the other foot back down. When he didn't and I lost my grip on his hoof and it came down on top of my foot, it was the most painfull thing I can ever remember. I fell to the floor and rolled away from him a screaming, and laid there for about fifteen minutes before I could get up.

After I was up again, went looking for a half of a cow hobble with a ring in it, and a soft cotton rope. I tied the rope around his neck and ran it down his back over his ass in the crack by his tail, then threw the ring on the hobble, and pulled the hoof up with the rope and tied it. Then every time he leaned on me I would step away from him and let him fall, after four times of falling he quit leaning. On the front leg I tied the rope around the other leg then ran it over his back then put the hobble on the one I was working on then tied it up, every time he leaned I would let him fall, he quit being hard to shoe.

* * * *

I was riding a colt for Jim Tew one year, one day we were gathering the bulls off the cows in Rawleea's mine area. I was trailing a bull on a road threw the timber, when he ducked by me and started running back. I got the colt to run up to him and I got the bull roped; about that time the road turned to the left. The bull ran straight into the trees, the colt turned left and followed the road, and I missed my dallies and lost my rope. The bull was going downhill through the timber and I knew I would not catch up to him on the colt. So I bailed off and took off running, after about a hundred yards of jumping down trees I got a hold of the rope. When I had enough rope I ran around a tree and stopped him then tied it off. When I walked back for the colt, Tim Tew was waiting there holding him. Tim was riding a big good horse so he handled the bull. We snaked the bull back up to the road then the three miles down to the corrals.

* * * *

The first year after calving when we started branding they sent three men over from White Sulphur Springs and hired two from Ennis do the roping. We had to do all the ground work. We would start at three in the morning; by day light we would about have the cattle gathered. Then the guys roping would show up to help corral them and sort the cows off. There was about five hundred head each time. We would do two bunches each day, we did close to three thousand head in three constitutive days, on the fourth day we picked up the last little herd, a couple hundred.

One day I was roping calves that got out while they we sorting the cows off. When I was dragging a calf back in, it ran behind the horse I was riding and got the rope under its tail, he went to bucking. After about six jumps I got ready to bail out, I got my left foot out of its stirrup and ready to jump, then I noticed that the rope would dump me on my head if jumped. So I sat back down and went to riding him out. I looked behind me and saw Mark Samson running behind the horse trying to pull the rope out from under its tail, the horse was kicking over and around Mark's head he finally did get the rope out and the horse stopped. In the four days we got up at three AM, branded all day, came home and team roped until nine, then went to the bars until two, then started all over again. This went on for three days, on the four when we were done branding we went to Kenny Prices for his horse sale, it lasted until six, then I went home and died. The next year we started only doing five hundred a day, and doing the roping our self.

* * * *

I bought a horse from Tim Tew, I think he was six years old, but looked old - when he was twelve he looked

250

young. I called him a catch all breed, which is what I call a horse that had a little of each breed. He stood sixteen hands, had real high withers that I had to have a special saddle pad for, a real small head, big flat front feet. He turned into a real good horse I headed and heeled on him, and Tom Davis hazed on him when I bulldogged. When he hazed on him, if he was not by the steer when I turned him, he would try to follow the steer. Once in bull dogging at the Lincoln rodeo when I got down and started the turn, Tom and the hazing horse were right on top of me and I had to push him away with my feet on his belly. Tom and I were at the Helmevile rodeo, in a three head team roping, we went into the third steer in first place. On the third steer we made a good run and had first place pretty well won, until we heard that barrier hadn't work. On the rerun we got the fastest steer that no one had caught in any decent time, he outran us so no money. I should have broke the barrier and taken the ten second penalty instead. I named this horse Biggin. I never had a horse that could walk down a hill as fast, it was like he would put it in neutral and let it roll. He had one bad habit: it seemed like once a year he would step in a gopher hole and piled up. But at least he always landed on his side with no rolls.

* * * *

Bob Cowins sent a small three year old gelding he bought at Kenny Prices horse sale to make into a kids

251

horse. He was a rank little bugger, and so small that when he would buck you couldn't see any front end. After a month of riding he was not getting any better .

Tim Tew, Tim Clark, adn I were at the Spring Ranch doctoring yearlings. Tew had one headed, and when I went for the heels the colt went in too high and I got my right foot over Tim's rope. When the yearling hit the colt in the ass he blew up, when he spun away from the rope my spur hung up and pulled me out of shape. After about three jumps I hit the ground. Clark went and caught him backup. We finally got the doctoring done, but he had ruined my record of not getting bucked off. I had been in a lot of wrecks but never been bucked off since coming to the Rock Creek Ranch.

* * * *

One year Steve Davis won the local team roping. I took second in the bull dogging at the Deer Lodge rodeo and won about two hundred dollars. After the rodeo a bunch of us went out for dinner and Steve and I payed the bill. When it was done, I didn't have enough to cover my entree fees for the next rodeo.

* * * *

A neighboring rancher sent me a big good looking black four year old gelding to ride - I was the third rider to get him. He was easy to handle until it was time to mount - then he got dirty. I had cheek him hard and get rough. He did try to buck but he was not that tough so we got threw it fine.

The first big job we did on him was when Tim Tew, Jack Liebee, Dave Stenson and I were trailing the bulls to Dog Creek for the winter. We were going up a ridge when a black bull cut from the herd ran into a timbered draw. Dave and I gave chase. We were going on a trail, and when he got to the draw he ducked to the left. That is when I roped him.

The colt kept running past the bull, so when the rope came tight it spun him around and we were standing on top of a four foot ledge. When Dave got there I gave him my rope because he was riding a big good horse. We started going up the draw making good time because the bull was running up the rope and hitting Dave's horse in the ass so we caught up with the herd in good time.

The next event that happened on this horse was when we were riding the meadow in sub-zero weather. I went to step off of him, and when my foot hit the ground the other one would not come out of the stirrup. I pulled on the left rein as he spun away from me, and jumped for the saddle horn. I was lucky and caught it and got back on.

I used him to ride calf lots doctoring. One day we were running on ice trying to head a calf when the calf fell down right in front of us. I have rode a lot of horses but I have never had another one do what he did. He

253

kept running, and somehow jumped sideways and ran right by the calf.

When I took the horse back I tried to trade Biggin for him.

* * * *

One morning when we were going to put yearlings through the chute I woke up with good case of the flu. I asked Tim if I could skip work today, but he said we were short-handed today and try to tough it out. So I went back to the bunk house and got out the cow combiotics, (and gave myself a shot). That was the first mistake, because it was slow to absorb and it left a bump. The second mistake was when I gave myself the shot in the cheek of my ass, so when I was in the saddle I was sitting on the lump it was rather irritating.

We got done about three o'clock. I had been running the head catch all day and one minute I would be freezing the next sweating. It was well below freezing that day. When the last one went through the chute I told Tim to unsaddle my horse when they were done, and I headed straight to bed. The next morning I was fine.

Another morning we were about to go riding and I had canker sores on the roof of my mouth. I grabbed a bottle of liquid we use for sterilization to rinse my mouth out with, but iodine comes in the same style of bottle and I got wrong one. After I rinsed with iodine I couldn't spit for two days - but it did get rid of the sores.

* * * *

A little before Christmas the first year out of high school I was up at Jim Tew's ranch on Grassy Mountain by myself taking care of things. One night I went out rabbit hunting about six, and a while later I got stuck.

I had drove across a snow filled draw and fallen through the crust. After getting the scoop shovel and digging down to ground beside the left front tire, the hub of the tire was eye level. It was around two o'clock in the morning by the time I had shoveled a path wide enough from the base of the front tires to where the snow wasn't too deep. Then I put the pickup in neutral, and got behind it. When I pushed it fell forward and the snow under it fell with it until its tires were on the ground. It was good thing the window was rolled down or I would have done a lot more shoveling to get in. I was one pooped puppy when I got to bed.

* * * *

That same winter on the second of January I went into a cow camp. There was me, five saddle horses, two Belgian draft horses, one wagon to feed with, one sheep wagon to live in, one old barn, one old shed, one big corral with no water in it, and 615 cows. The first day after I caked them I drove the team back alongside of the line and got a count - it was about thirty head short. So I finished feeding them with 100 bales of straw and 100 bales of hay. It was a good team of Belgians. They handled 1200 pounds of alfalfa pellets, two hundred bales of hay and straw in three loads. The next day I went hunting for the cows I was short.

I left way before first light, found them about 10 o'clock about five miles back in the hills. They were in a grove of aspens and two feet of snow, they looked pretty tough. It was about noon when I got back. I got lucky because Tim was there and he had gathered the pasture and had caked them so all we had to do was feed them the straw and hay. This camp was about fifteen miles east of the southern edge of Livingston I think it was called Harvard flats. About the sixth night the wind came up and the sheep wagon rocked up on two wheels. When it came down I came flying out of there in my shorts. It was about a month before I got use to that happening. The propane heater would not work so I had it taken to town to get it fixed - it was gone about a month and a half. So all the heat was a little cook stove. The fire in it would not last very long, at night it would get well below freezing in the wagon. Most nights I had to wear my Scotch cap with ear flaps down to keep my ears from freezing, I slept in down sleeping bag with a heavy down comforter over it. I have never slept better anywhere. In the mornings I would start a fire, put the coffee on, put the milk close to the stove to thaw, while I was saddling and harnessing the horses. After breakfast I would lead the saddle horse to the back side of the pasture which was about two miles. This was to thaw the ice in my boots and warm my feet. After I had gathered the cows in the four section pasture, I would feed them. This went on by myself for three months. I was glad they were a well broke team. I had several bad wrecks with them where I was starting to feed the bails off and hit a rock with a wheel, and threw me off onto the team. On the way down to the team, I would howler as loud an mean as I could to whoa. Every time they stopped and let me get myself untangled from the harness and get off them without moving.

One day while I was gathering I heard some different noises. I finally spotted about twenty turkeys walking in the trees. They would show up about twice a week, and if you would wait until they would walk out of sight then run after them I could get within a 100 feet of them. I thought about shooting one, but I would have had to clean it, and I could not figure out how to cook it in the little wood stove. It got so bad for entertainment I would crawl over the front of the wagon while the team was walking and lay down and let the wagon roll over me. I had to trail the horses about a mile up the draw to the springs to water every evening to water them. When the weather got nicer and they were feeling good, they were coming back from the spring running bucking, and jumping over cows laying on the feeding grounds. When one of the Belgian jumped over a cow as it stood up and sent the horse into wreck. When he got up he trotted off looking back over his shoulders like if to see if any one saw him fall.

* * * *

There was a good looking horse from the Benny Benion ranch and after I rode him I knew why they sold him. When he was in a lope and you tried slow him down he would run away until he got tired or came to a fence. About the first of April one man showed up to help with the calving. I pulled out of there in the middle of May, I really enjoyed that job.

* * * *

Mike Quin sent a five year old gray gelding over to Tew's to be broke. Tim started him, but after a week and Tim getting dumped twice, Tim and I decided to double him. So Tim would ride him one day and I would the next, he would get rode five days a week. This went on for about a month and a half. All we got was one smart horse that was in shape, and handled fair, but was always trying to get you. He never did stop trying to get us, and he got very good at it.

I finally inherited him. One day we were riding the neighbors looking for yearlings. I was riding down a ridge when he started in. He made about four jumps downhill then ducked to the left. He had me bucked off. I went down the right side of him, far enough to touch the ground with my right hand. But somehow I got back on top. I have never figured out how I stayed with him.

Later that day we found two yearlings and had to rope them to get them home. It was about three miles to the home pasture. After about a mile I had burned all the rubber off the saddle horn, and I had to tie the rope to the horn. The last two miles I had thirty five feet of rope between us, and the horse wouldn't step over the rope. When we got to the pasture I stepped off and dropped the reins hoping he would stay, I then went up and got my rope off. When I was almost back to the horse he took off running for the barn. The men working on the dude ranch saw what was happening and ran out to try and catch him. They turned around and ran back when I opened up with my pistol trying to kill him. The last time I rode him was to gather bucking horses. I rode him because I didn't want to ride one of my good ones. The day before the gather I ran him in from a two month rest, so I topped him off. He went at it hard.

The next morning we unloaded in a plowed field. When it was time to mount I had him cheeked hard and got stood up in the stirrup when he blew up. I just stayed standing in the one and on the one side of him. Before long he went down. I held his head back so he couldn't get up. After I got on him, I let him get up, then I made him run in the soft ground until the edge was off.

Later I was coming down ridge at a hard run trying to turn some horses, after they were turned, and I was slowing him down, I could feel him getting ready to tie into me. So I let him keep on running. I got lucky and he hit an old abandoned fence. He went into a skid but not a roll so he didn't get a chance at me. Lawrence Johnson took him for his son to ride when he caught him spurring his good horse in the shoulders. The horse finally ended up in the bucking string of a Wyoming rodeo contractor.

The last time we gathered Mike's horses was for his horse sale at the Four Dot ranch between Manhattan and Belgrade. When we unloaded we found the horses in the neighbor's stubble field. Orville Workman and I went to ride around them to open the gate to the lower pasture. The horses started running before we got there and broke through the gate to the big pasture.

They ran up the draw on the road. We went up a ridge trying to beat them to the top and turn them back. We were about five horses to late, so we got off and let our horses blow. When the last horse was by I fell in behind them to keep them moving so they would not scatter. Orville went back down the road to pick up any strays and tell them what I was doing. I was chasing about 100 head, going at a hard trot or a lope for an hour and a half. We finally came to the gate and some help - we were back to the same place it all started.

We trailed them down to the Clarkston railroad stock yards and left them for the night. The next morning we trailed down the road, across the river to Logan, then up the old highway through Manhattan, and on up to the ranch, I guess it was about thirty miles. I heard later that were only five head of horses short.

* * * *

Over Labor Day weekend Don Lewis, Dave Doig, two of Dave's friends, and I packed in to Scott Lake which is south west of Dillon. We took three pack horses and two saddle horses. When we got done packing the horses we did not have any left to ride. It took some time to get to the lake because there was no trail for horse and we had to make one. We were really going to rough it: there was two rubber rafts, a TV to watch the baseball game, and a radio to listen to the football game.

The meals were not what you would call rough: we had steaks, scallops, clams, salmon steaks, and a lot of other good food. When the first morning came the horses were gone, I picked up their tracks and started trailing them. After two miles, I found them in a park grazing.

After two days we had caught one fish, and that was with a gill net. It was a fun trip if not a good fishing trip.

* * * *

My dad located two steers Bob Davis was short. They were a long way from a corral, so not to run weight off them we decided to rope them and drag em in the trailer. We drove up close to them and unloaded my

261

horse. From the time I stepped in the saddle until the second steer was loaded, about fifteen minutes had passed. A week later a neighboring rancher told me he had been watching us and it made him nervous to see how easy and fast it would be to steal cattle.

* * * *

Tim Tew and I had a running bet one summer on roping Hereford bulls: who ever roped him had to have a clean horn catch, then the other had to pay two bits.

We were bringing a bull down a draw through Bill Murphy's pasture for Deer Park. When we were about half way down, I made a run at him. He was in some scattered trees going downhill. His horns were almost grown into his head, but I made a clean catch and drug him in the trailer. I so proud of that loop you would have thought I had won the national finals.

* * * *

Tim and I were riding the back country early one morning during hunting season, when we rode over a small rise with sun at our back and a little misty. We were right in the middle of about of thirty elk. When they started running, we were running with them.

I pulled my rifle and went looking for a bull. No luck finding one so I put the rifle up and got my rope ready. Tim was in front of me making a run at one, but Slick, the horse he was riding, was running blind. There was a calf running behind him, and after a little ways the calf turned off and jumped a fence. Once Tim got control of his horse again we rode on talking about another close chance of roping an elk.

* * * *

Tim Tew, John McNeil and I were riding the upper Little Black Foot river country looking for stray cattle. It was cold and we were in about two feet of snow. John was complaining about being cold, so we told him we would stop at the skiing lodge at Slade Lake for coffee.

When we got there and he saw it was a just an old fallen down log shack, and he had fallen for our con job, he called us some bad names. But it warmed him up and got him through the day.

* * * *

There was three head of yearling moose hanging together. One was blind, but the other two seemed to take care of him.

One day as we rode out of the timber we were real close to them, so we tried roping them. The blind one went out to the middle of a beaver pond and stayed, the other two ran for the trees about 100 yards off. We got close but not close enough.

Days later we saw they had got back together, Tim told the game warden about them, and he went up and shot the blind one.

* * * *

One day when I was on the haying crew Tim sent my wife Bernadette and me to the Gold Creek pasture to doctor yearling steers. I did the heading, Berne did the heels. We did about ten head in some pretty tough country. I don't remember her missing a loop. I really enjoyed that day.

* * * *

One year during calving Dave Wadsworth asked me to help him with a colt he had just back from someone starting. I rode him working new pairs out.

When he would get close to a tree or a fence, he would try to rub me off on it.

Later that day we trailed some pairs over to the Beck Hill pasture. As we were riding back he started running towards a twenty foot cut bank in the creek. I pulled his head around to my left knee but he didn't change directions. We were getting close to the bank and I was thinking of bailing out. But I tried jerking his head from my left knee to my right knee. It caught him off guard and he spun around.

I told Dave that this horse was a canner, but somehow Dave got Pickering to buy him for the ranch. Tim Tew got stuck riding him. One day while he was riding him back from Mannix Park he started running down the road in the timber. When they came to a park

Tim got him turned and running along a fence. He was leaning against the fence so hard trying to rub Tim off that he fell over it, when he landed on his side he had his feet caught in the fence and could not get up.

When we got there Tim was standing there thinking about killing him so he would not have to ride him again. He decided not to because he didn't want to carry his saddle back. I don't think that horse was rode any more.

* * * *

One summer day when I was still in high school Tim and Clay Tew, and I couldn't think of anything to do. We finally put our tenny-runners on, grabbed our ropes, and walked down to the bull pasture. We tied our ropes around our waists, herded some bulls against the fence, and each roped one by neck. Then we would sit on our ass and let them drag us until they would choke down, then we would get our ropes off. We did this twice, then had to think of something else to do.

We grew up with the belief that if you got close enough, you roped it no matter what it was.

* * * *

Just before school one year Clint, Tim, Weed and I packed into Edith Lake. We got camp set up and the horses picketed in a park. The next morning we saddled up and went exploring towards Baldy Lake, Gypsy Lake, and the Twin Needles.

After we got back to camp we saw some people coming hiking in over the ridge. When they got down we knew these people had a cabin on Deep Creek and they were heavy drinkers. They set up camp across the creek and up the hill.

After supper we went to their camp to visit and have a drink. After a few Clint and Clay left but Tim and I stayed and got plastered. When we left we must of looked like two balls from a pin ball machine the way we went down that hill bouncing from one tree to the next.

At the creek there was no way we were going to cross it like we did before by stepping from rock to rock, so we just waded across and hoped not to fall and take a bath.

The next day we loaded up with theirs and our stuff and packed out.

* * * *

The next year Tim, Clay, and I packed in again, but it was right after the 4th of July. Going in was hard. When we started down the trail into the crater, the trail was still snowed over and we had to make a new trail. It took some time.

After camp was set up we took the horses up to a park where we picketed 3 and hobbled 3, thinking that as tough as it was to get in there they would stick around. That evening the horse flies came out in force.

The next morning the 3 were gone, so we saddled up and went hunting. We trailed them up to the ridge and then lost their tracks. So we split up an went looking.

Around two I picked up their tracks an started trailing them. After a ways they were going back down the trail we rode in on, and they were on the tracks of Tim or Clay. They followed their tracks a ways then they left the trail and went straight down the mountain. I found them in a tight bunch of trees fighting the flies.

After gathering them up we headed back to camp. When back at camp I covered them completely up with tarps for relief from the flies, and not a one seemed to mind the tarp.

After breaking camp and loading everything I headed out. As we topped the ridge we ran into Clay. When we got to where the truck was supposed to be it was gone. Clay and I unloaded everything into the pickup and tied the horses to trees and headed to the ranch to get the truck. At the ranch there was no truck so we unloaded the pickup and headed for our first guess where Tim would be.

We headed for Rhonda Helmeek's house -Tim's girlfriend. We guessed right, so we traded outfits and went for the horses. That trip was a lot of work for no fun,

* * * *

One day while sitting at the table at Jim Tew's ranch we saw Clint Tew and Butch Mothershead come riding over the hill. All of a sudden they started galloping and swinging their ropes. The gray filly Clint was riding blew up and bucked him off. He went real high in the air, and he was running before he hit the ground. When they got to the house they told us that Clint roped a badger, and it ran up the rope and bit the filly on the heels. All Clint was thinking while he was in the air was getting away from the badger, so he started running before he hit the ground.

* * * *

Pickering sent a horse over from the White Sulphur Springs ranch and I got him in my string. He was a runner - I mean he would run and you couldn't stop him until he wanted to. I tried every bit I owned and every trick I could think of. One good thing was he would let you turn him so you had some control. I finally figured out that he if was a little played out he wouldn't run on you. So when I would get him in from a rest I would ride him every day until he quit running then use him twice a week. One of his worst runs was when we were coming down a ridge where there was a barb wire fence on my left side, the drop off on the right side that was too steep to ride, with about three feet between them.

When he started running, all I could do was let him run. As we came close to the bottom of the ridge we came alongside a jack leg pole corrals. Past that was very steep grades, so when we were going by the jack legs I jerked his head into one and piled him up.

He was a good horse to do work, with the exception of that one bad habit. I named him R.P. - the R, stood for real and I will let you guess what the P, stood for.

* * * *

One spring I was calving for Bill Higgins and when the calving slowed down I started breaking two filly colts for him in the spare time. The three year old was easy to break and train. After working her out I would ride her around the indoor arena at a walk to cool her out.

Cindy Higgen's Siamese cat was there, it had been kicked out of the house and sent to the barn. I got in the habit of picking it up and letting it ride on my lap. Later that summer Bill saddled a horse, and as he rode by the cat sitting on the fence, it jumped on the horse's ass and sunk his claws in. When he did the horse blew up and dumped Bill. The next time I saw Bill I sure heard about it with a few chose words.

Sundays I would take the pickup and pitchfork and clean the indoor arena of frozen cow pies. Then I would catch up the horses to rope on. I tried to catch Bill's horse and was having trouble so I ran him in the alley behind the barn. I was walking up the alley to catch him, when he came running at me. I was waving my arms and yelling to stop him. He wasn't slowing down so I jumped to get out of his way, but he swerved to go around me and I jumped right in front of him. I would say it looked like a seven, ten split when he was done runnin' over me.

Later that summer I was working the four year old full sister to the three year old, at ranch west of Ringling. She was easy to train but liked to buck each morning. One morning when I was ready to ride I took her out the back of the barn to a corral to top her off as usual. This time when she bucked she went off the bank into the creek, fell down, she got her head under water - and I never had any trouble with her bucking again.

* * * *

Corrine, Cindy, and I were riding back from moving cattle. Cindy had been bragging about how fast of a walker her mare was. I was riding the three year old daughter of her mare, and I was working the filly with my off foot so Cindy couldn't see me doing it. I was getting the filly to walk faster than Cindy's mare and it was starting to make her mad. Corrine thought it was funny and started ribbing Cindy about it.

I was a funny duck about horses, if I could train them to walk fast I could get along with about any horse, it didn't matter how bad they were, but if I couldn't get them to walk fast no matter how good they were they would irritate me.

* * * *

Bill sent me out to doctor a yearling steer that was blind in both eyes from pink eye. I found him in tall sage brush, and it took four loops to get him double hocked because of the brush. After I got him laid down and tied up, I gave him a shot of canned milk in a muscle like Bill told me. I had never heard of this before. I saw the steer a week later and it had worked.

* * * *

I had a little contest with the bears up Dog Creek - there is a wild raspberry patch in the buck pasture. For three years I only got a hand full of berries as the bears pretty well had them cleaned up before I would get to them. On the fourth year there were enough to give me a belly ache.

* * * *

I bought a three year old gelding from Tom Davis that he bought from Brainard. It was quarter horse, thoroughbred cross. I named him Sacket. The first time I rode him he blew up when we were moving calves. He had me bucked off - when I was about to come off and he quit and let me back on. The next spring we were gathering bulls at the Dog Creek ranch, I was riding him he was still in the snaffle bit. I had to rope a bull that was giving us trouble, I got the bull down against a fence and going in the right direction. We had stopped and were resting. All of a second Sacket blew up I never had a horse go higher in the air. He made several jumps then hit the end of the rope and quit. He turned into a very good horse and could walk with about any horse.

* * * *

We were riding Plymale's land behind the section house between White Sulphur and Townsend. I was riding a Thorobred X-race horse. He stood about 17 hands and when the sun was directly overhead he was so narrow he would barely cast a shadow, but he could really run in a straight line. I was riding in some tall sagebrush when I scared up a nice buck. He was close so I took after him to see if I could rope him. We were really gaining on him even though the horse was stumbling quite a bit. About the time we were getting close enough to rope, the deer would change course a little and when the horse tried to follow his body would, but the direction he was traveling in wouldn't change and it would get pretty hairy. I went through this twice, then we hit a down grade and he left us in the dust. Thinking back on it I was lucky not to have been in one big wreck. I always wondered how that horse did on a track in the straight line run.

* * * *

The first real tough colt I ever started was a three year old Jim had for his niece Jody, so we named

272

him Joda. We had him in the corral and Jim was instructing me on how to cheek him as I got him. On the first two times I didn't even make to saddle before he had me on the ground. The next two time I wasn't even trying to ride him, the fifth time I was a little mad and gave it try, the sixth time I was really mad and there was no way he was going to win this time. I always wonder if I set a record in getting bucked off five times in the least amount of time. He turned into a good horse.

* * * *

Don Shonka and I were gathering bulls out of upper Trout Creek one after noon and I was riding Scooter. It was going pretty good - we had about twenty bulls together. When I found a Hereford in the willows, he wouldn't come out of them, so I was chasing him around in them. We came to a spot where Scooter couldn't go any farther. The bull wasn't like a fighter, so I went to get off but there was no place to get off him on the left, and I forgot who was under me and stepped off the right side. When I did, Scooter jumped away and kicked me in the left ankle, I did manage to hang on to the rains. After he drug me a little he stopped.

After Don showed up we managed to get the bull in a little clearing and I got him roped, then we tied him to a tree. We left him there for the night and he led out with the others. It was well into night by the time we got home with them. The next morning Don took a pickup and a horse to get him. We tied him to the pickup and I put another horn loop on him to keep him from going around a tree. I needn't have bothered because Don went out of there so fast that all the bull could do was stay behind him, I couldn't keep up. When Don got to the road Howard Robbins and Tim Tew were waiting with a trailer so I got my rope back and drug him in.

* * * *

I acquired a big good looking horse in my string and he was well broke, Steve Davis had been using him doctoring in the calf lots. The ranch bought him from Bill Murphy. He was a nice ride except that at walk about ever fifth step he would stumble and most time he would go to his knees. When you looked at him hard you could see that his front legs were set back under his chest a little too far. It didn't seem to bother him at a trot or lope just the walk. I learned to touch lightly with my spur after four strides to remind him, to lengthen his stride, we got along fine from then on.

* * * *

A five year old Belgian was sent to Dog Creek ranch to replace one that was acting like he might go lame. He was big and gentle but there had not been much work done with him to train him. So Don Shonka and I start using him with the good horse on lighter loads, after about a week we decided not to tie their tails together when we drove them to the sled. That was a big mistake. When we were clear of the corral. he went to fighting his head and swung around toward each other and got the lines messed up. The lines were so I had no control of the good one and little control of the new one and he had control of the good one. When they started running all I could do was hang onto the lines and drag on my belly and hope I didn't meet a big rock in the three feet of snow.

I did have a little control in the right line so when we were going by a pole fence I manage to turn them into it, after we got them straightened out and hooked up I started taking my clothes off you wouldn't believe the amount of snow that can pack in to them doing that.

* * * *

When I was in the eighth grade I started bulldogging, the first time was at Bob Masola's on his horse Ginger. The first try I leaned forward and went off on my head. They told me that was wrong (no shit). The next time I leaned back adn I went right over the back of the horse and they told me that was not right ether (no shit I can of figured that out myself). The, third time I got down right and after that I could get down good; adn if I had ever figured out how to throw them fast I could have been pretty fair.

In the district high school rodeos at Townsend in four I years never missed a steer, hoolahanded two, which is when I got down my feet were too far to the right and when they hit the ground my feet didn't slid and the steer ran over me and we went into a roll but I never let go of it, so when we got stopped and stood up again and threw him, I got my time.

My senior year at district the first steer I got down right out of the box. This was the first time these steers had ever been used. When I hit the steer he set up real hard an when he came down his left horn slid down in the front of my pants. I went to jerking his head up trying to get it out, after a couple tries and no luck, I decided the hell with it and threw him no matter what might happen down there. Ever thing seamed to turn out all right, ended up with a time of 6.9. I think I must of wasted 2 seconds trying to save my man hood.

The next day on my second steer I had out every piece of clothes I could find on, I had been up all night partying and was freezing for some reason, I ended up with a time of 10 something and ended up in second place. At state finals in Malta I got down on both steers in good shape but they were so big that when my feet hit the ground they picked their heads up and carried me to the end of the arena there I got my feet in the fence and got them stopped and thrown. A big Indian lad won it. I heard later that he but was twenty three years old. I don't know if that was true. If so I weighed 160 and he had a good 50 lb. on me.

After the last show there was a big party in the camp grounds. This was the first year the legal drinking age was 18. It had turned that the week before and there was plenty of beer; it was legal this year for a change. At about one AM the bucking stock came running through the camp grounds - somebody had opened the gate to the rodeo grounds and ran them out. There were kids running over me trying to turn them back. Some of us got our horse and jumped on them bare back and went to trying to out run them before they got into town.

Me and two others headed them off just as they got to the edge of town. I. was on my bulldogging horse, we got them stopped and when more help showed up we put them back where they belonged. I had followed them in an when they had gone as far they could go they doubled back I could see them running at me an knew I wouldn't be able to stay on when they hit us so I got off and hid behind my horse. After they were by I got back on an rode back an threw them to the gate an out. A Stuckey girl and I found a bull in the rodeo parking lot and were really going all out when we got him back to the fence of the rodeo grounds and he went right through it. After it was all done the camp ground got real quiet. Everyone thought the cops would show up, but they never did.

* * * *

One Sunday Tim and I were coming back from riding at Bill Higgen's, when we met my dad as we were going up the Deep Creek canyon. He started flashing his head lights so we knew we were wanted. He had shot a bull elk and wanted us to drag it out, so we drove up to the place an unloaded our horses. There he guided us up to the snow where his tracks were. Then he headed back to the trucks and we followed his tracks for about two miles until we came to the bull.

I tied onto the head and Tim to the heels. We had to go along the hill side, so every time we came to a tree Tim would stop an dally up. When the elk would come back up to be behind me again he would slip his dallies until it was past the tree. Then he would trot up to get enough rope back to do it again. We made very good time doing it this way. By the time we got back to the trucks dad had just got his under a big limb and hung the pulley in it. He fed our ropes through it and we snaked it into the air adn he backed his truck under it. That was one of the easiest elk I ever handled.

* * * *

Tom Davis and I had been riding Dog Creek helping Don Shonka. On the way home we pulled down into Trout Creek and unloaded and went hunting. In about a half hour we jumped two nice bulls up out of their beds. I have never seen a person bail off there horse, jerk there rifle out of the scabbard, and get off a shot faster than Tom and still drop what they were shooting at.

When I went to pull my rifle out of the old borrowed scabbard I had it in, it would not let go. The other bull was getting way, so I forgot about the rifle and took after him with my pistol, but couldn't get close enough for a shot. When I got to Tom he had it dressed out so I hooked onto it and started down the mountain to the stock truck. We just drug it in with horse and headed for home. But first we had to stop at the Avon bar to celebrate, so it was rather late by the time we got home, unsaddled, hung it up and skinned.

* * * *

One spring day were pushing pairs to higher pastures, Howard Robbins our cow boss was having trouble with his dog Smokey. He was traveling out in front of Howard, and every time he called him back in a little while he would be back out there. After a while he would just look back when Howard called, and it wasn't long before he wouldn't even look back. You could see Howard getting ticked off. He then took down his rope an put the loop around the horn and let the 30 feet drag. The next time he called and got no response, he whipped it out with a under hand swing of the arm and it went like a bull whip. It caught the dog right in the ribs. He went down howling and biting at his ribs. About ten minutes later he caught up with us and he paid close attention to what Howard said the rest of the day.

I would guess that Howard hit about 80% of what he tried to pop, in 8 years of trying to learn it I got where I hit about 50% the other 50% I ether hit the horse in the ass, or myself.

* * * *

Am getting into an area of stories that I remember but don't know how correct or true they might be.

The first job I remember having it wasn't mowing the lawn - I wasn't big enough - it was being a cat skinner. When Dad and Grampy would have to track the D8 cat across a highway and I was handy they would line it up, put in low gear an idling, then put me in the seat to run the clutch. When ready I would pull it back and they would lay old rubber tires down for the cat to roll on. If they got behind in rotating the tires around, I would stop to let them catch up. When we were across I would stop and give it back. You would have thought I had just built the Alaskan highway the way I would strut around.

The next job I wanted was the summer I was going into the first grade and dad had leased some land from Harold Marks and planted sugar beets. I wanted to ride on the harvester and use a machete to cut the tops off any beets that were missed. This is where it turned into a con job on me.

Mom and dad told me that a person couldn't do that if they had tonsils. So I got in a hurry to get the little suckers cut out. Looking back I was sure was gullible, but I did get a little Chihuahua pup out of it - more about him later. I did get to be on the harvester a little and whack at some beets.

* * * *

I was like a pup when hunting season came around. Where ever dad went I was sure to try to follow. One morning up around the Eagle Creek Ranger Station we were about three hours from the pickup when we jumped some elk. We took after them, and in ten minutes dad could see I couldn't keep up so he stopped an let me catch up. He asked me if I thought I could find my way back to the truck by myself. He asked if had my hunting knife, hatchet, an my shotgun shells full of stick matches (which was a used 16 gage shell with matches packed in it with a used 12 gage shell put on the other way to protect them). He told me if I got lost to stop and build a fire and he would come and find me.

It was a long and spooky trip but I did make it back to the truck, and I graduated from pup to dog. After that I was given firecrackers and sent out to scare game while they would set around and waiting for me to scare something out to them. I even got to pack the 22 rifle with dad to shoot grouse before I was of age.

* * * *

When I was little I tried to always be around when dad came home from work. You never knew what he might have in his lunch pail. It might rabbits, birds, or anything surprising. One winter day he brought a doe deer home he found down on the ice of the river and laid it in the utility room. It stayed there a long time warming up. I got real close to it and pet it and it didn't move. When dad went to turn it loose I tried real hard to talk him into keeping it as a pet.

* * * *

In the vacant lot across the street from our house dad took the cat and dozed up banks for a ice skating rink. He put a shack, and a pole to hold the loud speaker for music. The first afternoon he put water in it I couldn't wait to try it out, so after I went to bed I snuck out and went on it. Ever thing went fine until I got to the deep end then down I went through it. It was only three feet deep but it was hard getting out of it. But the real hard part was getting back to bed without getting caught or leaving signs of what I had been up to.

* * * *

Now most kids have a swing, but few had one like mine. When dad wasn't using the drag line he would park it at the house, take the bucket off and put a swing on it. We would tie a rope to it and give each other high rides. Every now and then dad would start it up an give us rides above the house, and when a car would drive by that he knew wouldn't get mad, he would lower us and let us tap on their roof. We sure did startle some people. The first time I got to ride on it when he lifted me up I wasn't heavy enough to come back down. So dad had to get out on the boom adn pull cable out to get me down. After that my cousin that was a year younger than me would sit on my lap facing the other way to make enough weight. My uncle had built a house on my ice skating rink.

* * * *

One year at the fish derby below the Toston dam while walking along the river, I found a hurt little baby water snake. So I picked it up by the tail and carried it about two hundred yards back to where the derby camp was. On the way it would curl up around my hand and try to bit me. I am glad that when the Gerdler kids had caught a garden snake we had learned that little snakes had a hard time getting to you if you shaked them when they curled up at you. When I got to the camp I walked up to Grampy and showed him the snake I had with the smashed tail. When he saw it he said I might want to get rid of it because you got yourself a nice little rattle snake. After that I was a little more careful about what I picked up.

* * * *

The winter I was in the third grade the family was logging up North Fork. When spring started they couldn't haul logs during the day because the roads got to soft.

With hauling at night they couldn't get enough loads in so they had to work weekends. Mom and I would go up to stay with dad right after school on Friday. When the truck come in dad ran the loader. Uncle Moose, who drove the truck, would put the tongs on the log. After dad swung the log on I would walk down it to unhook them. We would do three or four loads a night. On one load, when we were most of the way done, I released the tong and the log shifted and trapped my thumb. It didn't hurt, but I couldn't get loose to get of the way for the next log. I went to screaming for help but no one could hear me over the engine noise. I started waving my other arm hoping someone would see it. About the time dad started another log for the truck I was getting close pissing my pants. Before that happened dad saw me and stopped, then Moose got a bar and came up and pried the logs apart. After that I was a little more careful.

* * * *

I would do this Friday and Saturday nights. On Saturday and Sunday I would help dad skid logs with the John Deer rubber tire skidder. I would ride on the engine and hang onto the support bars of the roll cage. We would have to go the long way around because it was too steep to climb with all the moisture. When we were at the top I would get off and pull some cable out and hook the end choker up to a log in the snow. Then dad would drive down the hill a little, feeding the cable out. He would park and help me crawl around in the snow hooking chokers on, then we would get back on the J.D. and start winching the logs up.

Sitting on the engine hood then was like sitting on a bucking horse, but now I hung onto the exhaust pipe to dry my gloves out and warm my hands up. After the logs were drug up to the piles and unhooked, we got to do it again. Some times when the driving was real easy he would let me drive. Those weekends were a blast.

* * * *

The dog I got for my tonsils we named Smoky. One day while driving in the mountains he went nuts in the truck. After about half mile we came around a bend and there was a herd of elk standing in the road. Before we could get a hold of Smoky he bailed out the window and took after them. In a few minutes we seen the elk going through a park across the draw. They would trot a little ways, stop, and look back. We could see a little black dot coming after them and hear the bell on his dog collar. We started calling for him and honking the horn. After fifteen minutes we about gave up getting him back, but then we heard his bell and seen him running through the park again.

He had a very good nose. Going to Helena in the car with the windows up he would go nuts, and after several miles we would go by some Antelope. One day hunting birds on the back side of the Hogbacks, someone downed one. We could not find it with about ten people adn Bud Sautter's high priced bird dog looking. After looking quite a while we gave up adn started loading up. When we were about ready to go and went to load Smoky, he was not to be found. We finally heard his bell and found him under a big sagebrush wresting with the bird. It was bigger than him.

* * * *

We spent a lot of time in the pickup driving on the dirt road. When my older sisters got older there wasn't much room for five in the front seat. On the pickup box dad had built tool boxes down each side, and then a top for it. He ran a rope across the front and down the left edge of the topper. After we got off the highway he would let us get on top and lay there hanging on to the rope while he drove. Donna always got the left front corner, Dorothy got right front corner, and I always got stuck behind Donna on the left side. I didn't get to see much because it went by too fast, so I usually fell asleep. But I always made sure my left arm and leg were wrapped around the rope so if I should slide off I would hang up.

* * * *

Dad helped trail Mike's bucking horses from Clarkston to Townsend when I was in the fifth grade. When they got in there was a yearling colt that wasn't supposed to be there. While they were trying to figure out what to do with him, I asked dad if we could buy him.

286

He said yes, and told me to go and talk to Mike. When I asked Mike how much he wanted for him, he asked me how much money I had on me. I told him I only had twenty bucks on me. He said he would take ten for him. And that was my first horse trade. When I sold him it was a sure bet I would make a profit.

* * * *

The summer before high school I worked for Hubert Plymale, his dog bit me hard right at the beginning and was always trying to get me all the time. So when we would go up to the Section House to do work and it would get out of the truck, I wouldn't tell Hubert that it hadn't got back in when we went home. In two or three days he would get home, then he would lay up resting for a couple days. It was nice not having to be on the watch for him.

One day Hubert sent me out on the motorcycle to run a two year old Angus bull in to haul up to the heifers. It was no trouble finding him, but half way to the corral he turned on me and knocked the bike down. I just stood on the other side and kept standing it back up to keep something between us until he left. Then I went back and got a horse - what I should do in the beginning.

One day while haying it rained, so we were taking it off. Hubert gave me a little TV to take to the little camp trailer I slept in. When I walked up to it with the TV in my left hand and grabbed the door handle with my right I learned the trailer wasn't grounded. I will tell you it is hard to open one hand and not the other when there is 110 running through you, but I was not going to drop that TV. It felt like it took several minutes to release that door knob. I am glad we used to play a game with a hand crank from old telephone. A bunch of us kids sit in a circle holding hands and see who would be first to let go when dad would start cranking it. I learned it will not bother you as much if you hang on real tight until you're ready to let go. I always thought that game save my life.

* * * *

In my sophomore year dad and I went hunting Thanksgiving Day, we went up Cabin Gulch. It was after dark when we started back for Thanksgiving supper. When we had drove up the road we hadn't realized it was icy. On the way down we started sliding. It was right down the middle of the road so we weren't too worried - dad said when the truck gets to edge of the road there should be gravel. But when the road crossed a draw an dcurved the truck went straight and there was no gravel, so we went off the road in to the creek. It was a straight ten foot drop and the truck landed right on the radiator, but with dad's homemade grill guard there was no front end damage the head lights were not even broken. When the front end hit I slammed on to the windshield but that was a good thing because the inch drive socket set for the cat was on the floor boards, an if I hadn't been between it an the glass when it hit we would have lost the windshield. The pickup box had the side tool boxes on so the roof wasn't hurt too bad when it rolled onto its top, but the 200 hundred gallon gas tank in the back was leaking bad. So dad got engine turned off real fast, when he had crawled out he went in the back and turned the gas valve off. When I was able to crawl out tmy window I landed in the creek's water. We then dug out some cable, heavy duty come along and started to roll the truck. We got it on its side an just before it was about roll onto its wheels the come-along broke and it rolled back to its side. So we hide the guns up in the trees, an started walking out. We found out the road was covered with ice all the way to the highway. In the several of miles of road to the highway I must of fell 20 times, then had to walk several more miles down the highway to the Deep Creek Bar - there never was a car that went by. We got a ride to town - mom wasn't nerves yet about us being late. The next morning Jack Sautter took us up to roll it over, then hunting the rest of the day. That evening we went back an scraped motor oil off the window, put oil in it and drove it home.

* * * *

Around the first of March my junior year dad had some land surveyed, then took me out there and told me how to read the stakes, then showed me how to use a hand eye level with the measuring stick. After that he

289

said have at it, so on weekend an days I would skip school I climbed on the Caterpillar self-propelled scraper and try to level that ground. It didn't take long to learn that it was easier to take your time and do it right than go back correct mistakes. It was dam cold when I started on this job, so we put plywood down the side of the engine and the seat to direct some heat back to me, but I still had so many clothes on I looked like a big ball. When it got warm and the bees came out, and the dust would gather with the diesel fumes on the fuel tank right next to me, those bees would go nuts for that stuff. When they would get too thick and start crawling up my arm I would stop and bail out of there adn wait until they had eaten it all up, then start again. We would go through this two or three times a day. While I was doing this dad was on the other side of the creek building a fish pond with the cat and can [D8 Cat and Pull Scraper] when he got done he sent me about five miles over to MacArthur's to pick up loads of bentonite in my scraper to line the pond to help stop leaks. The bentonite was on a hillside so on the way up you would get half of the load, but the turn around on the hill side for the other half was spooky. The scrapper would tip onto three wheels in the turn and if you didn't keep the cutting edge close to the ground it might have rolled. When I was bringing the fourth load back I could see we had company parked in the yard. I trying to see who it was, and not paying attention to what I was doing. When I came to the turn off I was going too fast, and when I turned it only made a parcel turn because I didn't have the motor turning over fast enough to keep the hydraulics running. So we were headed for the irrigation canal. There was no way the brakes would stop it in time, and the only thing I could think of was to drop the cutting edge. When I did it came to a stop in two feet and we had ten feet to spare. It was a good thing the steering wheel was there because the stop stood me up and it was all that kept me from going out over the front. When I got everything straightened out I had very large divot to fill in. It was very scary way to learn to pay attention to what you are doing.

Right after I got done leveling the field the irrigation system showed up, the first part we buried there was lots of room so dad decided to try the ditcher he had made. When he had made it the first time he used it the D8 Cat pulled the tongue out of it so he had to rebuild it. The next time he could go deep enough to make the cat spin its tracks. The first trip went real good but the next one the ditcher kept jumping around, so we went got the old International tractor and tied it to the back of the ditcher and I would ride on it using the brakes to hold it in place. We did that trench in about three hours, it would have taken a good two days with a backhoe. The rest was a lot slower. It was next to fences so had to use a backhoe.

Later that summer Dad had job over on the Smith
River north west of White Sulphur Springs. Dad was
hauling the cat on the lowboy, and I was pulling the can
behind a 3/4 ton 4 wheel drive pickup. Going up Deep
Creek Canyon wasn't too bad - just had to watch out for
room. Thirty or thirty five miles an hour was all I was
comfortable with. I was doing real good until we came to
going down the hill just past the Section House. When I
started down it I was in first gear and creeping along. It
wasn't long before I had to shift to second when the can
started pushing the back end of the pickup around to the
side. It wasn't long before I was in third gear. B the time
we were to the bottom it was close to 70 miles an hour -
all I could do was stay in front and try guide it. The big
old heavy tires on the can were really hot by the time I
finally got it stopped. Later when I was about a 1/3 of
the way up a long dirt road on fairly steep hill a gas truck
waved me to stop and told me Dad had asked him to stop
and gas my pickup up. When he was done and I tried to
take off the truck did a lot of wheel spinning to gain a
foot and I didn't have any tire chains with me, ad I knew
I couldn't back down the hill adn get another running
start at it. By the time we got to the top I was surprised
there were any tires left on the pickup.

* * * *

One summer dad got the job of piling the trash off
a logging site for a winter burn up Crow Creek. He was

292

using International TD25B dozer which was a lot bigger than the old 60s D8 Cat. Things were going good until it turned hot out, then it broke down, and had to get a mechanic out of Billings for two days. It cost a thousand dollars for him to replace a 25 cent O-ring. Later that summer he came home and told me to get Sparky in to pull the dozer out of a spring he had ran into and got stuck. The next morning we hauled up there. While I was saddling up he unloaded 30 feet of 2 inch cable and tied a rope to it. I drug it several miles up hill to the dozer, it was in the mud almost to the top of the tracks. I was still trying to figure out how we were supposed to get it out, when he took one end of the cable and put it around a big tree an hooked the other end to the tracks on one side. Then he drove that side up the cable until it was on good ground, and then did the other side.

That fall Dad had a job leveling land up close to Toston. When he was about done he got another job across the river leveling for someone else. So after changing sprinkler pipe from 6am to 10am then I would go to Toston and work at finishing that first job, then back to the farm at 4 to change pipe till 7. I had just finished the Toston job and the irrigation when dad got dust pneumonia so I went out to work on the new job. I had never leveled land with the D8 Cat and Can so Grampy came out to help me get started. After about 4 hours I figured I had it handled so when the bucket was full this time I hit the fuel lever and the up lever for bucket. But as usual I goofed up. I pushed the fuel lever the right way but not so on the bucket lever. The cut edge went about 3 feet in to the ground, and before I could get the Cat stopped the cable that raised the bucket broke. I was glad that Grampy hadn't left because he had to show me how to rethread it - it took over 2 hrs. to get back up and running. So when I went back to leveling the land again I went back to operating it like the true beginner I was.

Beginning of the End

****

Jim was a neighbor of mine on the Shields River who loved his horses. He had a handful of the stoutest, prettiest bunch of buckskins I'd ever seen. But early into the New Millennium he was cussing when he called me to shoe one of them.

"I've got to get in a cow from up in my summer range and I can't get there on my four-wheeler."

****

"I haven't saddled a horse in two years", said Pol, a rancher I had worked with years before in the Bear Paw Mountains.

"First you buy a four-wheeler to do the irrigating, then you figure out how good it will work to run in the horses."

"Then one day you realize that you could be there and back on the four-wheeler in less time than it would take to get your horse in and saddle it. That's the beginning of the end."

"And when you really need a horse, he's so fat and out of tune that you can't get the job done any way. And then it's all over".

****

****

I have told in this book the story of having used a pickup and slide-in stockrack to retrieve a stray cow. That pickup was two-wheel-drive and had a second-hand motor; I don't recall what I traded for the stockrack. I used the horse to corral the cow and then hauled them both back home in the pickup. Thirty years later I watched the same sort of operation take place across the way with a new generation rancher.

He and his wife had driven out to a bunch of cattle away from their headquarters, in a diesel quad-cab 4wd pickup equipped with a hydraulic round-bale feeder, and carrying an All Terrain Vehicle. Just their equipment was worth as much as 30 cows.

They had cut out a critter of some description and were bringing it back to the corral. She led the way in the pickup, with him following the beast in the ATV. Amazingly to me, they got the job done!

From there, they loaded the ATV on the pickup, drove back home, and returned with the stock trailer that was worth another 5 cows.

***

For most folks, ranching isn't about cows - it's about a lifestyle. And for me, that lifestyle is about horses.

There is no money in *raising* cows – the profit comes only when you sell the ranch. But who wants to <u>sell</u> the ranch!?! The joy in ranching comes from riding a good horse – one who understands what you want to accomplish, and who puts his heart into accomplishing it with you.

Horses can only maintain their cow-working skills when they are used, and even in the New Millennium we still use horses regularly: to cut out heavies, to check the cows, to cut out pairs, to doctor, to bring cattle into the shed or corral, to sort cattle, to brand, to move to new pastures, to fix fence, to check cattle on summer range. There are plenty of jobs that can still be done faster, cheaper, easier, and better on a horse.

Kenny Doig, Steve Gordon, and I are three out of many cowboys in Montana who have lived our lives with our horses. But horseback ranches are rapidly becoming a thing of the past. My local barber estimates that fewer than 10% of the ranches in the Livingston area use horses more than a couple of times a year.

At least *I* am still doing my part to keep horses as a vital part of the ranch. And even when the weather is miserable and everything seems to be going wrong, as long as I am ahorseback there is nowhere else on earth that I would rather be.

Ain't This Romantic!??

About the Author

Kent Hanawalt has spent more than 40 years working with horses and cattle in Montana – as a cowboy, fencing contractor, horseshoer, wilderness guide, muleskinner, horse trainer, ranch manager, and camp cook.

After twenty years of making his living on the ranches of North Central Montana, his cowboy career was pulled up short by a wreck with a team of horses - he had broken his back!

Lying there in his hospital bed he had plenty of time to think. After all those years making his living with his back, it was now time to start using his head. Three months later he was able to sit up long enough to begin classes at the College of Great Falls.

Kent achieved his Bachelors in Business Administration the same year that his oldest daughter graduated from Montana State University - and spent the fall riding for a large ranch south of town. Ten years later he received a Masters in Business Administration from the University of Montana - and hurried back from the graduation ceremony to trail the cows to summer range.

Now deeply involved in the management and operation of the 114-year old Ellison ranch, Kent still shoes his own horses – and some of the neighbors. He uses those horses year-round to accomplish tasks that are impossible on the modern "Japanese Quarter Horse".

Join him now – at the ranch, or through his writings - and explore the depths of the romance, adventure, knowledge, and just plain hard work that go into ranching in the Big Sky Country of Montana.

http://mellinniumcowboy.blogspot.com/

http://www.montanacowboycollege.com

64176699R00188

Made in the USA
Lexington, KY
30 May 2017